"IT 英语"系列教程

中级IT英语
听说教程 ① （第二版）

总主编　司炳月
主　编　刘　欣
副主编　刘晓静　郭　鹏
编　者　刘可欣　王晓华　王　豪
　　　　崔梦雪　李泽雨　曹　麟
　　　　张婉婷　于　芳　张雅欣

清华大学出版社
北京

内 容 简 介

本书共有 16 个单元，每个单元分为 Section A、Section B 和 Section C 三大部分。其中，Section A 注重听力技能的培养，包含听力热身活动及与单元主题相关的精听练习，题目设置由易到难；Section B 注重口语技能的训练，并设有相关的口语活动；Section C 为听力强化训练，以便学生进一步练习和巩固听力技巧，题型多样，题量丰富。本书每个单元均配有听力音频及单元小测，读者可先扫描封底的"文泉云盘防盗码"解锁资源，再扫描书中对应处的二维码，通过"文泉云盘"获取音频资源，通过"文泉考试"进行单元测验。

本书适合作为 IT 相关专业和科技英语专业学生的英语听力教材，也可作为从事 IT 相关工作人士提升英语听说技能的参考资料。

版权所有，侵权必究。举报：010-62782989，beiqinquan@tup.tsinghua.edu.cn。

图书在版编目（CIP）数据

中级 IT 英语听说教程. 1 / 司炳月总主编；刘欣等主编. -- 2 版. -- 北京：清华大学出版社，2024.7 (2025.6重印).
("IT 英语"系列教程). -- ISBN 978-7-302-66783-4

Ⅰ. F49

中国国家版本馆 CIP 数据核字第 2024N45K85 号

责任编辑：刘　艳
封面设计：李伯骥
责任校对：王荣静
责任印制：刘　菲

出版发行：清华大学出版社
网　　址：https://www.tup.com.cn, https://www.wqxuetang.com
地　　址：北京清华大学学研大厦A座　　　邮　　编：100084
社 总 机：010-83470000　　　邮　　购：010-62786544
投稿与读者服务：010-62776969, c-service@tup.tsinghua.edu.cn
质 量 反 馈：010-62772015, zhiliang@tup.tsinghua.edu.cn
印 装 者：大厂回族自治县彩虹印刷有限公司
经　　销：全国新华书店
开　　本：185mm×260mm　　　印　　张：13.75　　　字　　数：315 千字
版　　次：2017 年 11 月第 1 版　2024 年 9 月第 2 版　　印　　次：2025 年 6 月第 2 次印刷
定　　价：69.00 元

产品编号：104146-01

第二版前言

一、改版背景

随着《国家中长期教育改革和发展规划纲要（2010—2020年）》和《大学英语教学指南》（2020版）的深入实施，我国高等教育迎来了新的发展机遇和挑战。为积极响应国家对于优化学科结构、促进多学科交叉融合以及培养复合型、应用型人才的需求，我们在保留第一版教材优势与特色的基础上，深入教学一线调研，广泛征询意见，对教材进行了全面升级与改进，以更好地服务于新时代的高等教育改革和人才培养目标。

二、修订思路

本系列教材主要修订思路如下：

1. 更新与拓展教材内容

第二版教材在内容上进行了大幅度的更新与拓展。选材紧扣"人与科技发展"的主线，引入了更多前沿科技话题，如人工智能、无人驾驶、数字时代等，使教材内容更加贴近时代发展步伐，让学生更加了解行业背景，拓宽知识视野。

2. 有机融入课程思政元素

遵循《高等学校课程思政建设指导纲要》的精神，第二版教材每个单元都穿插了与中国传统文化紧密相连的内容，通过介绍中国科技发展的辉煌成就，潜移默化地培养学生的文化自信、爱国情怀和社会责任感。此外，教材还通过具体实例，如对重大科技创新项目的介绍，引导学生深刻体会科技进步对国家繁荣和社会进步的巨大推动力。

3. 注重将技巧讲解与任务型训练相结合

第二版教材注重将口语技巧讲解与任务型训练相结合。任务型训练的设计具有真实性、实用性、挑战性和互动性，使学生在完成任务的过程中能够运用所学专业知识和口语技巧，不断提升语言运用能力。例如，在公共演讲部分，教材提供了详细的演讲稿结构和功能性口语表达大纲，引导学生通过模仿和练习，逐步掌握公共演讲的技巧。

4. 满足个性化教学需求，促进教师专业发展

第二版教材充分考虑了学生的个性化学习需求，也为教师提供了丰富的教学资源和灵活的教学选择，教师可以根据具体教学情况和学生需求自主选择教学内容和活动形式。

同时，在备课过程中，教师也能够对自身知识结构进行反思，及时更新教学理念和教学方法，在教学实践中不断成长和提高。

三、教材结构

第二版教材经过精心设计和编排，旨在全面提升学生的英语听说能力，特别是在IT领域的专业英语沟通能力。本系列教材由《初级IT英语听说教程》和《中级IT英语听说教程》组成，每个教程包含两册，每册精心编排了16个单元。《初级IT英语听说教程》以通用英语为主，旨在夯实和提高学生的英语听说基本技能。《中级IT英语听说教程》以IT英语为主，旨在培养学生在IT场景中的英语交流沟通能力和跨文化交际能力。

《初级IT英语听说教程1》中每个单元的内容设置遵循时间和逻辑上的先后顺序，话题选择贴近学生的真实学习和生活。在口语技能训练方面，第1至3单元注重培养学生开展对话的能力；第4至7单元注重培养学生的口语思辨能力；第8至13单元注重培养学生日常交流中的语用能力；第14至16单元主要培养学生的情感输出能力。同时，依据各单元的主题和难度递增原则，教材还配有相应练习题来巩固本单元的听说技巧。

《初级IT英语听说教程2》则融入了IT学科特点，侧重英语的实用性和应用性，逐步实现通用英语向专门用途英语的过渡。教材内容既有个人发展、交流技能、工作效率、时间管理、团队建设等与职业发展基本素养有关的主题，也有社交媒体、网络安全、人工智能、云计算等与计算机网络有关的主题。每单元的口语技巧训练包含四个活动：第一个活动以听力的形式训练学生捕捉关键信息的能力；第二个活动要求学生复述听力材料；第三个活动以任务式教学为依托，以问题式提纲为索引，引导学生通过素材的收集与整理找到问题的答案；第四个活动通过小组互动，互帮互促，最终以演讲的形式呈现指定话题的相关成果。整个教学过程不仅有助于学生听说能力的提升，而且可以使其循序渐进地提升口语表达能力，增强其学习动力和兴趣。

《中级IT英语听说教程1》作为初级教程的延续与深化，旨在进一步提升学生的英语听说能力。每单元由三个部分组成。第一部分注重听力技能的训练，通过两个导入性问题引导学生关注本单元的主题，再加上一系列由易到难的听力练习，帮助学生熟练掌握和提高听力技能，同时更好地理解与单元主题相关的IT知识。第二部分专注于口语技能的训练，培养学生的公共演讲能力。每单元包含一个公共演讲主题，配有相关问答题及体现本单元公共演讲技能的演讲稿，并通过大纲填空的方式使学生熟悉这类演讲的结构和功能性口语表达，最后引导学生完成一个符合本单元公共演讲技能要求的演讲，锻炼其公共演讲能力。第三部分为听力强化训练，共包括三组听力练习，内容涵盖学习、生活、职场等各个方面。

《中级IT英语听说教程2》与IT场景紧密相关，各单元主题划分清晰。第1至5单元关注人工智能与网络技术对日常生活和学习产生的影响；第6至13单元聚焦数字时代的新发展；第14至16单元是对计算机网络技术发展与社会和人之间关系的深度思考与展望。在口语部分，教材除了对口语技巧进行细致讲解外，还设计了大纲填空和主题演讲练习，使学生能够学以致用。听力强化训练部分的题目设计服务于学生参加各类国内外英语考试的需求，并围绕同一主题提供全方位的语言输入，拓展学生视野，引导学生完成多样的听力和口语活动。

四、教学建议

第二版系列教材包括教师用书、练习答案、听力脚本、教学课件等丰富的教学资源，为实施分级教学、分类指导与创新教学模式提供了广阔的选择空间。针对第二版教材的特点和使用需求，我们提出以下教学建议。

1. 针对学时有限的课程设置：对于英语听说课程学时较少的学校，建议教师在 Text A 和 Text B 中精选一篇文章作为主要教学内容。通过这篇文章，教师可以引导学生学习和掌握关键的听力技巧，并将这些技巧运用于深入理解听力材料。同时，公众演讲和听力强化训练部分的教学内容和活动可以采用课堂教学与课后作业相结合的方式进行，确保学生在课外也能继续练习和巩固所学知识。

2. 针对学时充足的课程设置：对于英语听说课程学时充足的学校，建议教师在课堂上完成单元所有内容的教学。每个单元的教学内容可以在两周内完成，这样的安排既能保证教学的连贯性，又能给予学生足够的时间来吸收和应用新知识。此外，教师可以根据具体的教学安排和进度，将部分单元练习题作为课后作业，并在随后的课堂教学中进行检查和评估。这样的做法不仅有助于教师检验教学效果，而且能够培养学生的自主学习能力和团队协作精神。

在本系列教材的编写过程中，我们经过了多次研讨和反复修改，力求使教材内容更加完善和实用。本系列教材的编写团队由具有多年 IT 英语教学经验的大学一线英语专业教师组成，他们丰富的教学经验和专业知识为本系列教材的编写奠定了坚实的基础。同时，我们也感谢清华大学出版社和大连外国语大学软件学院在编写过程中给予的大力支持。

由于编者水平有限，教材难免存在问题与不足，在此也欢迎各位专家、读者在使用本系列教材的过程中提出宝贵的意见和建议，以使教材不断改进和完善。

司炳月
2024 年 9 月

第一版前言

一、编写背景

1.《国家中长期教育改革和发展规划纲要（2010—2020年）》

信息时代的悄然而至，使得我国教育在面临难得的改革与发展机遇的同时，也面临着全新的挑战。传统的教育理念、教学模式、教学内容、教学方式、教学手段、教育结构乃至整个教育体制都将随之发生变革。2010年，教育部颁发了《国家中长期教育改革和发展规划纲要（2010—2020年）》（以下简称《纲要》），《纲要》中提出要"优化学科专业、类型、层次结构，促进多学科交叉和融合。扩大应用型、复合型、技能型人才培养规模"。在对创新人才培养模式的论述中提出，要"加强教材建设，确定不同教育阶段学生必须掌握的核心内容，形成教学内容更新机制"。

2.《全民科学素质行动计划纲要实施方案（2016—2020年）》

2016年3月，国务院办公厅印发了《全民科学素质行动计划纲要实施方案（2016—2020年）》（以下简称《方案》）。《方案》中对高等教育中的教材要求有清楚的阐述："加强各类人群科技教育培训的教材建设。结合不同人群特点和需求，不断更新丰富科技教育培训的教材内容，注重培养具有创意、创新、创业能力的高层次创造性人才。将相关学科内容纳入各级各类科技教育培训教材和教学计划。"

3.《大学英语教学指南》

《大学英语教学指南》（以下简称《指南》）是新时期普通高等学校制定大学英语教学大纲、进行大学英语课程建设、开展大学英语课程评价的依据。《指南》在对教材建设和教学资源的论述中明确阐述了："鼓励各高校建设符合本校定位与特点的大学英语校本数字化课程资源；鼓励本区域内同类高校跨校开发大学英语数字化课程资源。"

二、编写原则

本套教材是与IT及其相关专业密切相关的知识课程配套教材，符合新形势下国家对复合型人才培养提出的要求，符合语言学习规律和新时代大学生的认知水平，也满足大学生专业学习和未来职业发展的实际需要，有利于促进复合型人才培养目标的实现。本套教材在设计与编写过程中遵循以下原则：

1. 满足社会对于复合型人才培养的需求

当代大学生正面临多元化社会带来的冲突和挑战，复合型人才的培养成为国家、社会发展的需求。因此，为社会提供既具有专业知识又具备跨语言交际能力、能够直接参与国际交流与竞争的国际化通用型人才是高校人才培养的重点和难点，也是全球化对人才提出的更高、更新的要求。

2. 满足学生对于专业与外语知识相结合的需求

高校开设大学英语课程，一方面满足了国家、社会发展的需求，为国家改革开放和经济社会发展服务；另一方面，也满足了学生专业学习、国际交流、继续深造、工作就业等方面的需要。本套教材旨在满足 IT 及其相关专业学生的需求，帮助他们在掌握专业知识的同时提高英语水平。此外，教材亦体现了专门用途英语理论对大学英语教学课程设置的具体要求。

3. 满足大学英语教学大纲和教学目标的要求

大学英语的教学目标是培养学生的英语应用能力，增强学生的跨文化交际意识和交际能力；同时发展其自主学习能力，提高综合文化素养，使他们在学习、生活、社会交往和未来工作中能够有效地使用英语，满足国家、社会、学校和个人发展的需要。本套教材编写的目的就是使学生能够在 IT 专业领域中使用英语进行有效的交流；能够有效地运用有关篇章、语用等知识；能够较好地理解有一定语言难度、内容较为熟悉或与本人所学专业相关的口头或书面材料；能够对不同来源的信息进行综合、对比、分析，并得出自己的结论或形成自己的认识。

三、编写依据

1. "专业知识"+"外语能力"的"复合型"人才培养目标

大学英语课程作为高等学校人文教育的一部分，兼具工具性和人文性。在进一步提高学生英语听、说、读、写、译基本能力的基础上，学生可以通过学习与专业或未来工作有关的学术英语或职业英语获得在学术或职业领域进行交流的相关能力。本套教材是根据大学英语教学大纲和教学目标的要求，采用系统、科学的教材编写原则和方法编写而成。从教材的前期策划和准备、单元设计、教学资源开发、编写团队、内容设置和编排到教学效果的评价和评估都有整体的体系构建，以满足教学大纲和课程目标的要求。教材不但注重培养学生听、说、读、写、译这些语言基本技能，而且强化学生思辨、创新能力的培养。

2. "学生为主体"+"教师为主导"的"双主"教学理念

《指南》中提出大学英语教学应贯彻分类指导、因材施教的原则，以适应个性化教学的实际需要。新一轮的大学英语教学改革中也明确提出了"以教师为主导，以学生为主体"

的"双主"教学理念。在教学过程中,教师的主导作用主要体现在课堂教学设计、教学组织、教学策略使用、教学管理和协调、课堂教学评价和评估等方面,而教师对课堂的主导方向要以满足学生的个性需求、促进学生的个性发展和自主学习为目的,只有两者相互结合,方能相得益彰,顺利实现大学英语教学改革目标。

3. "语言输入"+"语言输出"的"双向"驱动教学体系

本套教材在课堂教学活动和课后练习中设计了很多"语言输入"和"语言输出"的互动环节,教材采用任务式、合作式、项目式、探究式等教学方法,体现以教师为主导、以学生为主体的教学理念,使教学活动满足从"语言输入"到"语言输出"的需求。课后练习的设计关注学生自主学习能力的培养,引导和帮助他们掌握学习策略,学会学习;促使学生从"被动学习"向"主动学习"转变,真正让学生成为学习过程中的主体,实现课内和课外学习"不断线"。

4. "平面教材"+"立体化教材"的"双辅"交互优势

本套教材将大力推进最新信息技术与课程教学的融合,凸显现代学习方式的自主性、移动性、随时性等特点,发挥现代教育技术的推介作用。积极创建多元的教学与学习环境,利用互联网等信息基础设施和网络交流平台,使"平面教材"呈现出信息化教育的特征,成为"立体化教材"。

此外,本套教材鼓励教师建设和使用微课、慕课,拓展教学内容,实施基于"教材平面内容"和"网上立体课件"的混合式教学模式,使学生朝着主动学习、自主学习和个性化学习方向发展,实现教学资源网络化、教学环境虚拟化、教学个性化、学习评估过程化等目标。

5. 以教材为引导推动教师的自主专业发展,实现"教""学"相长

《纲要》明确指出,要"严格教师资质。提升教师素质,努力造就一支师德高尚、业务精湛、结构合理、充满活力的高素质专业化教师队伍"。教师的专业发展能力受多种主客观因素的影响,需要外在环境和管理机制的保障。教师专业发展的规律性特点可归纳为长期性、动态性、实践性和环境依托性。本套教材的编写和使用正是根据实践性和环境依托性的特点,编写和使用新教材的过程也是教师更新教学理念、提高教学技能的专业发展必经过程。

四、教材结构

本套教材共包含"读写"和"听说"两大系列。其中,"读写"系列分为初级、中级、高级三个级别,共六个分册。"听说"系列分为初级和中级两个级别,共四个分册。

在"读写"系列中,每册书有 8 个单元。每个单元分为 Section A 和 Section B 两部分。Section A 根据大学英语教学大纲的要求编制,包含一篇精读课文,课文后有生词表、短语和表达、缩略词、术语和课后练习。Section B 是按照专业英语学生的培养目标和要求编写，包含一篇与 Section A 同主题的阅读文章，旨在补充和强化专业阅读内容。两篇文章一易一难，每个单元都可以满足分级教学的需要和不同程度学生水平的需求，两个部分的练习形式多样，具有丰富性和系统性的特点。练习设计遵循语言学习的规律，针对不同层次、不同年级的学生，选材的难易程度、知识侧重点等方面均有所不同。

在"听说"系列中，每册书有 16 个单元，每个单元分为 Section A、Section B 及 Section C 三部分。其中，Section A 为听力技能训练，听力内容围绕 IT 相关主题展开。该部分由 Text A 和 Text B 两部分组成，前者针对 IT 及相关专业（非英语专业）学生，题目设计相对简单；后者针对英语专业（如科技英语专业）学生，题目设计难度有所增加。Section B 为口语技能训练，旨在培养学生的口头交际能力。Section C 为听力考试强化训练，该部分侧重应试，根据当下国内外几大英语考试（如大学英语四六级、托福、雅思等），全方位、多角度满足学生对英语学习的需求。教材希望通过题型多样、题量丰富的强化训练，让学生一方面熟悉并适应听力考试的多样题型，另一方面检测自己的英语听力水平，提高自主学习能力。

五、教材特色

1. 素材原汁原味

本套教材的所有阅读和听力文本均选自英美国家真实的 IT 专业文本，包括 IT 相关专业的学术网站、期刊及英语原版教材。编者在选择文本时尽量选择新颖、有趣的分支话题，文章的语言也尽量避免过于严肃和刻板，使学生在理解和分析课文的过程中既能利用专业知识进行思考和判断，又不感觉枯燥。

2. 内容注重实用性

本套教材的"读写"系列避免了国内同类教材培养目标单一、片面的缺陷，注重提高学生的多种技能。每个单元不仅包括阅读板块、翻译板块和写作板块，还针对 IT 及其相关专业的英语阅读、翻译、学术写作等技能进行系统的讲解和训练。而在"听说"系列中，编者在选择听说文本的话题时，一方面迎合当今 IT 产业就业的发展趋势，另一方面也考虑与高校 IT 专业课程紧密相关，并参考国内各大重点高校 IT 专业设置，挑选出 IT 领域相关的热门话题，这些话题广泛涉及 IT 相关专业学生所关心的 IT 就业方面的问题、IT 专业知识的学习方法、全国重点高校 IT 相关专业课程中开设的典型编程语言、当今的网络环境、时下 IT 领域多项前沿技术等内容，以便在提升学生英语语言能力的同时了解和学习与 IT 相关的专业知识，突出语言运用，通过文本传递 IT 知识，重现真实 IT 场景。

3. 练习内容和形式丰富多样

本套教材在阅读和听力理解、语言知识学习及技能训练方面都设计了大量的练习，而且练习形式富于变化，如简答、判断、填空、选择、配对、翻译、图表、口语交际等，学生不仅可以学习词汇、短语等语言点，还可以提高阅读和听力理解能力、分析语言的能力及表达能力。

六、适用对象

本套教材特别适合计算机科学与技术、信息管理与信息系统、软件工程和网络工程等与IT相关专业的学生学习和使用，可以分阶段或分学期选用；也特别适合从事软件系统需求分析、设计、开发、测试、运行及维护工作的工程师和管理人员查阅和参考。编者在选材上保证与IT信息技术密切相关的同时，努力确保文章内容贴近生活，所选材料涵盖了当前教育、工作和社会领域的诸多热点，文字形象生动、可读性强。因此，本套教材也比较适合那些有一定英语基础，同时也喜爱计算机应用技术和互联网文化的人士阅读，以扩展知识，开拓视野。

七、编写团队

本套教材由大连外国语大学软件学院教师担任主编团队。参与编写的编者有来自全国各高校的大学英语教师、专业英语教师、计算机专业的教师、IT职场的企业专家以及旅居海外的专家和学者。

本套教材在编写过程中得到校企合作教材编写组的大力支持，在此表示衷心感谢。校企合作编写组成员包括李鸿飞、王文智、姜超、韩参、蒋振彬、梁浩、刘志强（排名不分先后）。

本套教材在编写过程中也得到了大连外国语大学软件学院的领导与英语教研室所有老师的鼎力支持，在此表示感谢。

由于编者水平有限，错误与缺点在所难免，恳请读者批评指正。

司炳月

2017年6月

Section A Listening

Page	Unit		
1	Unit 1 Computer Science	Text A	An Introduction to Computer Science
		Text B	Learning of Computer Science
11	Unit 2 Coding	Text A	Binary
		Text B	Dynamic Programming Language and Statically Typed Languages
23	Unit 3 IT Career	Text A	A Career in Field Services and Cyber-Services
		Text B	IT Expertise with a Specific Industry
33	Unit 4 Blended Learning	Text A	Free Online Learning
		Text B	The Benefits of Blended Learning
45	Unit 5 IT and Gender Disparity	Text A	Digital Technology and Gender Equality
		Text B	Women in the IT Industry
57	Unit 6 Network Security	Text A	Disregarding of Network Security
		Text B	Security Flaws of the Internet
69	Unit 7 Cyber-Attack and Cyber-Bullying	Text A	Cyber-Crime
		Text B	Online Attack
81	Unit 8 Data Theft	Text A	XcodeGhost
		Text B	Data Theft of Yahoo

Contents

Section B Public Speaking	Section C Further Listening
Introduction to Public Speaking	**Exploration Tasks** **A Glimpse of Chinese Culture**
Selecting a Topic and a Purpose	**Exploration Tasks** **A Glimpse of Chinese Culture**
Analyzing Your Audience	**Exploration Tasks** **A Glimpse of Chinese Culture**
Supporting Your Ideas	**Exploration Tasks** **A Glimpse of Chinese Culture**
Organizing the Body of a Speech	**Exploration Tasks** **A Glimpse of Chinese Culture**
Beginning and Ending a Speech	**Exploration Tasks** **A Glimpse of Chinese Culture**
Outlining a Speech	**Exploration Tasks** **A Glimpse of Chinese Culture**
Using Language	**Exploration Tasks** **A Glimpse of Chinese Culture**

			Section A Listening
Page 95	Unit 9	Internet Addiction	Text A TikTok Addiction Text B Screen Addiction
Page 107	Unit 10	Digital Economy	Text A An Introduction to the Digital Economy Text B The Role of Digital Economy in Transforming Business
Page 119	Unit 11	Technology and Work	Text A Transforming the Workplace by Technology Text B The Influence of Automation and Technology on Work
Page 133	Unit 12	Big Data	Text A The Advantages of Big Data Text B The Application of Big Data
Page 145	Unit 13	Algorithmic Bias	Text A An Introduction to Algorithmic Bias Text B Ways of Avoiding Algorithm Bias
Page 157	Unit 14	Artificial Intelligence	Text A Risks from Advanced Artificial Intelligence Text B Unlocking the Potential of Generative AI
Page 171	Unit 15	ChatGPT	Text A An Introduction to ChatGPT Text B The "Limits" and "Off Limits" of ChatGPT
Page 185	Unit 16	Digital Darwinism	Text A The Age of Digital Darwinism Text B Tendency Under the Digital Darwinism

Glossary 199

Contents

Section B Public Speaking	Section C Further Listening
Delivering a Speech	Exploration Tasks A Glimpse of Chinese Culture
Using Visual Aids	Exploration Tasks A Glimpse of Chinese Culture
Speaking to Persuade	Exploration Tasks A Glimpse of Chinese Culture
Speaking to Inform	Exploration Tasks A Glimpse of Chinese Culture
Speaking to Motivate	Exploration Tasks A Glimpse of Chinese Culture
Speaking to Demonstrate	Exploration Tasks A Glimpse of Chinese Culture
Speaking in Competitions	Exploration Tasks A Glimpse of Chinese Culture
Speaking on Special Occasions	Exploration Tasks A Glimpse of Chinese Culture

Unit 1
Computer Science

Learning Objectives

In this unit, you will:

- acquire basic knowledge of Computer Science;
- learn to grasp key information of a passage;
- get to know public speaking.

Background

The study of Computer Science encompasses a wide range of topics, including programming languages, data structures, algorithms, computer architecture, operating systems, databases, networks, security, artificial intelligence, machine learning, and more. With the rapid growth of the digital economy, Computer Science has become one of the most in-demand fields, offering exciting career opportunities in a variety of industries. A solid foundation in Computer Science is essential for anyone looking to succeed in today's tech-driven world.

Section A Listening

Pre-Listening

Work in pairs and discuss the following questions.

1. What is Computer Science?
2. What are some of the key challenges facing the field of Computer Science today?

Activity One

Match the words in Computer Science (1–5) with the definitions (A–E).

1. Applet	A. A set of instructions that a computer follows to perform a task
2. Program	B. A Java-based intranet program
3. Network	C. A group of interconnected computer systems
4. Algorithm	D. The process of finding and fixing errors or bugs in software
5. Debugging	E. A step-by-step procedure for solving a problem or achieving a goal

Unit 1 Computer Science

While-Listening

Text A An Introduction to Computer Science

Language Bank

effectively	[ɪˈfektɪvli]	adv.	有效地
immense	[ɪˈmens]	adj.	巨大的
practical	[ˈpræktɪkl]	adj.	实际的
prove	[pruːv]	v.	证明
investigate	[ɪnˈvestɪgeɪt]	v.	调查
laboratory	[ləˈbɒrətri]	n.	实验室
considerable	[kənˈsɪdərəb(ə)l]	adj.	相当多的
sponsor	[ˈspɒnsə(r)]	v.	赞助
deliver	[dɪˈlɪvə(r)]	v.	传递

Activity Two

You will hear a course introduction to Computer Science. Listen and choose the best answer to each question.

1. Which of the following basic questions related to Computer Science challenges is NOT mentioned in the passage?
   A. How can we catch in a precise way what we want a computer system to do?
   B. Can we mathematically prove that a computer system does what we want it to do?
   C. What is the most effective way to learn Computer Science?
   D. What are the limits to computing?

2. What does the Computer Science course focus on?
   A. It focuses on creating more cutting-edge systems.
   B. It focuses on creating relations between theory and practice.
   C. It focuses on introducing technologies and applications.
   D. It focuses on developing math abilities.

3. What type of work will students be expected to do during the first part of the course?
   A. Practical sessions in the laboratory.
   B. Discussing ideas with experienced computer scientists.
   C. Working on their chosen individual project.
   D. Attending lectures and tutorials.

4. In which year of the course will students take part in a group design practical session?
   A. The first year.
   B. The second year.
   C. The third year.
   D. The fourth year.

5. Who delivers the tutorials, classes, and lectures in the Computer Science course?
   A. Postdoctoral researchers and postgraduate students.
   B. World-leading experts in their field.
   C. Industry professionals.
   D. A mix of experts, postdoctoral researchers, and postgraduate students.

Activity Three

Listen to the passage again and complete the answers to the questions with ONE WORD ONLY.

1. What is the practical application of emerging Computer Science theories?
   The theories that are now emerging to answer these kinds of questions can be immediately applied to design new computers, programs, networks and systems that are transforming _____, business, _____ and all other aspects of life.

2. What kind of ability are the course organizers looking for in students, and what can it be used for?
   We are looking for students with strong _____ ability, which you will develop into skills that can be used both for reasoning rigorously about the behavior of _____ and computer systems, and for applications such as scientific computing.

3. What skills can you get and what do the majority of the subjects feature?
   You will also gain practical _____ and program design skills; the majority of subjects within the course are linked with _____ work in our well-equipped laboratory.

4. What is the expectation for students during tutorials in the Computer Science course?
   In tutorials, you will discuss ideas in depth with an experienced computer scientist, usually with just one or two other students. You will be expected to spend a(n) _____ amount of time developing your own understanding of the topics covered in lectures, answering questions designed to check your understanding, and _____ for tutorials.

5. What happens as the course progresses?

As the course progresses, you will also begin to work in small classes of up to _____ people on more specialized topics. Class sizes may vary depending on the _____ you choose.

Text B Learning of Computer Science

📞 Language Bank

decent	['diːsnt]	adj.	相当好的
vacancy	['veɪkənsi]	n.	空缺
prevailing	[prɪ'veɪlɪŋ]	adj.	流行的
mindset	['maɪndset]	n.	观念模式
conference	['kɒnfərəns]	n.	会议
take into account			考虑

🎧 Activity Four

You will hear a lecture about learning Computer Science in college. Listen and complete the notes below within three words in each blank.

I. Advantages

◆ Numerous companies only hire people who have 1. _____.

Some companies demand employees must graduate from schools like Princeton, Cornell or 2. _____.

Many companies do not take into account employees' 3. _____ and skills.

Getting an education in college may offer students more 4. _____ that self-taught people may not get.

◆ Colleges provide students with a(n) 5. _____.

Universities help students make a(n) 6. _____ with famous companies and provide them with resources that students might not have access to on their own.

II. Disadvantages

◆ The most obvious one—7. _____.

College education is really expensive, especially for some popular majors such as 8. _____.

Living on campus is expensive. Renting your own 9. _____ also costs a lot.
- The second drawback is time.
  College takes a(n) 10. _____ of four years.
  Some activities in school will not directly benefit students.

Activity Five

Listen again and decide whether the following statements are true (T) or false (F).

(   ) 1. Companies tend to label people into two categories: degree or non-degree.
(   ) 2. In the writer's opinion, some companies are pretty short-sighted.
(   ) 3. Nowadays, many schools may offer internships for their students; some companies even recruit directly from schools.
(   ) 4. Everyone knows that a college degree is really expensive, especially for some popular majors such as Information Analysis and Information Management.
(   ) 5. All the activities and time in school will directly benefit students.

Post-Listening

Work in pairs and discuss the following questions.
1. Have you ever enrolled in a vocational school?
2. Do you think self-study is necessary? why or why not?

Section B Public Speaking

Activity One

Read the passage below and get some knowledge about public speaking.

Introduction to Public Speaking

What is public speaking? Basically, it's a presentation that's given live before an audience. Public speeches can cover a wide variety of different topics. The goal of the speech may be to educate, entertain, or influence the listeners. Often, visual aids in the form of an electronic slideshow are used to supplement the speech. This makes it more interesting to the audience. Over the years, public speaking in communication has played a major role in education, government, and business. Words have power to inform, persuade, educate, and even entertain the audience. And the spoken word can be even more powerful than the written word in the hands of the right speaker.

The truth is that speaking in public is a skill. And you can learn any skill. While some people may have more natural speaking ability than others, anyone can learn to be a better public speaker. It just takes some know-how and some effort.

First, write an effective speech. The first thing you'll want to do is work on writing a well-organized, engaging speech. Because only having a great speaking voice or a great deal of charisma isn't enough if your material isn't any good. Second, overcome the fear of speaking. Fear of public speaking is real and can hold you back if you let it. If you don't feel confident when giving your speech, your audience may pick up on that. This can make your presentation less effective. Last but not least, practice the speech. Even if you're not afraid of speaking in public, practice helps you give a more effective speech. If you're in a rush, you may be tempted to skip practicing your speech to save time. Practicing your speech improves your public presentation skills. It also increases your familiarity with the presentation.

Activity Two

Answer the following questions according to the passage above.

1. How does the passage achieve the thematic ends?
2. What is the truth about public speaking? And what does it mean?

Activity Three

Fill in the blanks and complete the outline below according to the passage.

Public Speaking	
Definition	It's a(n) 1. _____ that's given live before an audience, which can cover a wide variety of different topics.
Goals	It may be to 2. _____, entertain, or influence the audience.
Effects	It played a major role in 3. _____, government, and business.
Skills to be a good public speaker	First, write a(n) 4. _____ speech. Second, 5. _____ the fear of speaking. Third, 6. _____ the speech.

Activity Four

Give a speech related to artificial intelligence by using the information about public speaking above. Your speech should address the following questions.

- What is the main advantage that AI has over humans?
- What is the main advantage that humans have over AI?
- Is it threatening to further develop AI? Why or why not?

Section C Further Listening

Activity One

You will hear five people talking about their work. Which of the benefits and incentives is each person referring to?

1st speaker	1. _____	A. Parental leave
2nd speaker	2. _____	B. A company car
3rd speaker	3. _____	C. A pension
4th speaker	4. _____	D. Flexible working hours
5th speaker	5. _____	E. An impressive job title

Activity Two

You will hear two long conversations. Listen and choose the best answer to each question.

Conversation One

1. Why is the man watching television?

    A. He's taking a break from studying.

    B. He has already finished studying.

    C. He was assigned to watch a program by his professor.

    D. He's finding out some information for a friend.

2. Why does the woman want to study linear algebra with the man?

    A. She did poorly on a recent test.

B. She thinks the man has studied linear algebra well.

C. She thinks they may study more efficiently if they work together.

D. She wants to help the man with his linear algebra.

3. Why doesn't the man want to call Elizabeth?

   A. He and Elizabeth argued recently.

   B. He doesn't want to bother Elizabeth so late in the evening.

   C. He heard Elizabeth did poorly on the last test.

   D. He'd rather study in his own dormitory.

Conversation Two

4. What does the man want to do after he graduates?

   A. He wants to become a cook.

   B. He hopes to go on to graduate school.

   C. He wants to travel around the world.

   D. He'd like to work at a hotel.

5. What was the woman's major in the university?

   A. Computer Science.

   B. Engineering.

   C. French.

   D. English.

6. Where does the man work part-time?

   A. At a bakery.

   B. In a library.

   C. At a restaurant.

   D. At a travel agency.

Activity Three

Listen to a passage on Chinese culture and fill in each blank within three words.

Xi'an

In the 7th century, Xi'an was the greatest city in the world. Half a(n) 1. _____ people lived there, whereas the biggest European city only had a few 2. _____ . It was a(n)

3. _____ place of new styles, new fashions, and new music. The city was said to be laid out like a vast 4. _____ board.

　　Xi'an was strictly 5. _____. That was the way Chinese cities have always been. Gated 6. _____ enclosure, where public access is controlled. Xi'an had 108 walls, all of them under 7. _____. This was the unseen world in the Tang Dynasty, between this area and great 8. _____ area over there. There were mansions of top 9. _____. A princess lived down the road. It looks like one can still buy some of that garden 10. _____ of them.

Unit 2

Coding

Learning Objectives

In this unit, you will:

- acquire basic knowledge about programming languages;
- learn to exclude useless information;
- learn to select a topic and a purpose for a public speech.

Background

Programming languages are essential tools used in computer programming to communicate instructions to computers. They provide a set of rules and syntax that allow developers to write code and create software applications, websites, and other digital solutions. As technology continues to advance, new programming languages are continuously being developed to address emerging needs and challenges in the software development industry. Mastery of programming languages is crucial for programmers and developers to effectively create innovative and efficient solutions in our increasingly digital world.

Section A Listening

Pre-Listening

Work in pairs and discuss the following questions.

1. What do you know about programming languages?
2. Are there any tips you want to give to someone who is starting to learn programming? What are they?

Activity One

Choose the best answer to each question.

1. Which of the following is NOT a programming language?
   A. Python.
   B. HTML.
   C. JavaScript.
   D. Microsoft Word.

2. Which programming language is often used for data analysis and scientific computing?
   A. Java.
   B. Python.
   C. C++.
   D. PHP.

3. What is the purpose of a programming language?

   A. To write letters and documents.

   B. To communicate with computers and give them instructions.

   C. To browse the Internet.

   D. To play video games.

4. Which programming language is primarily used for building web pages and applications?

   A. Java.

   B. CSS.

   C. PHP.

   D. Swift.

5. What does the term "coding" refer to?

   A. Creating algorithms.

   B. Designing user interfaces.

   C. Writing code in a programming language.

   D. Testing software for bugs.

While-Listening

Text A Binary

Language Bank

binary	['baɪnəri]	n.	二进制
transistor	[træn'zɪstə(r)]	n.	晶体管
voltage	['vəʊltɪdʒ]	n.	电压
volt	[vəʊlt]	n.	伏特（电压单位）
oscillate	['ɒsɪleɪt]	v.	（使）摆动
string	[strɪŋ]	n.	一串，一行
modulation	[ˌmɒdjə'leɪʃn]	n.	调制
bit	[bɪt]	n.	比特（二进制信息单位）

Activity Two

You will hear a lecture about binary. Listen and choose the best answer to each question.

1. Why do computers use binary code?

    A. It is a reliable way of storing data.

    B. It is a complex language.

    C. It is easy to understand.

    D. It allows for faster processing.

2. What is the main memory of a computer made of?

    A. Binary code.

    B. Voltage levels.

    C. Transistors.

    D. Software instructions.

3. What are the voltage levels that transistors switch between in a computer's main memory?

    A. 0 volt and 1 volt.

    B. High and low voltage levels.

    C. 5 volts and 0 volt.

    D. Oscillating and stable voltage levels.

4. How can the meaning of a binary sequence be determined?

    A. By its length.

    B. By the context in which it is used.

    C. By its position in the sequence.

    D. By the number of 1s and 0s it contains.

5. How is the sound in videos stored in binary?

    A. By using compression formats.

    B. By assigning each sound to a specific binary string.

    C. By oscillating voltage levels.

    D. Through pulse code modulation.

Unit 2
Coding

Activity Three

You will listen to the lecture again. Decide whether the following statements are true (T) or false (F).

(　　) 1. Transistors in a computer's main memory can switch between multiple voltage levels.

(　　) 2. Binary code is a pre-determined language with a specific meaning for each sequence.

(　　) 3. Context is not necessary to interpret the meaning of a binary sequence.

(　　) 4. Binary code is used to store complex types of data, such as sound in videos.

(　　) 5. The amount of binary data can be reduced through compression formats.

Text B　Dynamic Programming Language and Statically Typed Languages

Language Bank

compatible	[kəm'pætəbl]	adj.	兼容的
framework	['freɪmwɜːk]	n.	框架
momentum	[mə'mentəm]	n.	冲力
debug	['diːbʌg]	v.	调试；除错
reliability	[rɪˌlaɪə'bɪləti]	n.	可靠性
component	[kəm'pəʊnənt]	n.	组成部分；部件

Activity Four

You will hear a passage about the dynamic programming language JavaScript. Fill in each blank with ONE WORD ONLY.

Dynamic Programming Language

Not to be 1. _____ with Java, JavaScript is a primarily 2. _____ scripting language used for front-end development. JavaScript is compatible across all 3. _____ and is used to create interactive web apps, often through 4. _____ such as jQuery and front-end frameworks such as AngularJS, Ember.js, React, and more.

JavaScript can now also be used as a(n) 5. _____ language through the Node.js platform, and while Node.js is relatively new, the community is gaining a lot of 6. _____. You can also build 7. _____ mobile apps with JavaScript through using 8. _____ such as PhoneGap, while Facebook's React Native aims to allow you to build native 9. _____ apps with JavaScript.

However, JavaScript is also known to be a difficult language as it is 10. _____ and thus is difficult to debug. There are statically typed versions such as Microsoft's TypeScript or the JSX that React uses.

Activity Five

You will hear a passage about the statically typed language. Listen and match the following items with four programming languages marked A, B, C and D.

> A. Java   B. C   C. C++   D. C Sharp

( ) 1. It is often used to program software.
( ) 2. It is a general-purpose language and 90 percent of Fortune 500 companies use it.
( ) 3. It takes complex code to perform simple tasks.
( ) 4. It runs primarily on Microsoft Windows.
( ) 5. Facebook has developed several high performance and high reliability components with it.

Post-Listening

Work in pairs and discuss the following questions.

1. Do you want to be a professional IT engineer? Why or why not?
2. What essential qualities are needed for a professional IT engineer?

Section B Public Speaking

Activity One

Read the passage below and get some knowledge about selecting a topic and a purpose.

Selecting a Topic and a Purpose

Step 1   Choosing a topic

The first step in speech making is choosing a topic. Usually, the speech topic is determined by the occasion, the audience, and the speakers' qualifications. Most of your speech assignments will not come with a designated topic. You need to select the topic yourself. There are two broad categories of potential topics: subjects you know a lot about; and subjects you want to know more about.

◆ **Subjects you know a lot about**

Most people speak best about subjects with which they are most familiar. When thinking about a topic, draw on your own knowledge and experience. Everyone knows things or has done things that can be used in a speech.

Think for a moment about unusual experiences you may have had or special expertise you may have acquired. One student, who grew up in Turkey, presented a fascinating speech about daily life in that country. Another used her knowledge as a jewelry store salesperson to prepare a speech on how to judge the value of cut diamonds. A third student, who had lived through a tornado, gave a gripping speech about that terrifying experience.

◆ **Subjects you want to know more about**

You may decide to make your speech a learning experience for yourself as well as for your audience. You may choose a subject about which you already have some knowledge or expertise but not enough to prepare a speech without doing additional research. You may even select a topic that you want to explore for the first time. Say, for example, you've always been interested in Stonehenge but never knew much about it. This would be a perfect opportunity to research a fascinating subject and turn it into a fascinating speech.

Step 2 Determining the general purpose

Along with choosing a topic, you need to determine the general purpose of your speech. Usually it will fall into one of two overlapping categories—to inform or to persuade. When your general purpose is to inform, you act as a teacher or lecturer. Your goal is to convey information clearly, accurately, and interestingly. Your aim is to enhance the knowledge and understanding of your listeners—to give them information they did not have before. When your general purpose is to persuade, you act as an advocate or a partisan. You go beyond giving information to espousing a cause. You want to change or structure the attitudes or actions of your audience.

Step 3 Determining a specific purpose

Once you have chosen a topic and a general purpose, you must narrow your choices to determine the specific purpose of your speech. The specific purpose should focus on one aspect of a topic. You should be able to state your specific purpose in a single infinitive phrase (to inform my audience of…; to persuade my audience to…) that indicates precisely what you hope to accomplish with your speech.

Notice how clear the specific purpose statement is. Notice also how it relates the topic directly to the audience. That is, it states not only what the speaker wants to say but also what the speaker wants the audience to know as a result of the speech. This is very important, for it helps keep the audience at the center of your attention as you prepare your speech.

Activity Two

Answer the following questions according to the passage above.

1. How should a speaker choose a topic?
2. What are the two general purposes of a speech and how do they differ?
3. What is the importance of stating a clear and audience-focused specific purpose statement in a speech?

Activity Three

Read an example of a speech and complete the outline of it.

Hi, everyone. My name is Shou and I'm honored to have the opportunity to speak with you today.

This is a very special moment for you and your entire family. I still vividly remember sitting in your seats 16 years ago as a graduate of the Economics Department. I want to take a few moments today to share a few things I've learned on my own journey. Growing up in Singapore, a small island state, I knew that I wanted to see as much of the world as possible. Being a UCL and living in London gave me a diverse and international experience. Like many of you, I made some amazing lifelong friends from around the world during my time at UCL. After graduation, I didn't really know what I wanted to do or where life would take me. In hindsight, there was no big plan. I worked hard with what I had. I put myself out there, and I took chances when they came.

My first job out of college was to join Goldman Sachs, an investment bank in London. There I was introduced to DST, a young investment firm that had only just started. I didn't really have any investing experience then but I kept trying to learn and pushed myself to leave my comfort zone. I met many Internet founders during this journey, including the founding team of ByteDance and TikTok, and many years later, I found myself taking my current role at TikTok. Somewhere in the middle of this journey, I chose to go to business school in the U.S. I remember struggling with this decision, wondering if this decision would enhance or delay my career. I'm glad that I did choose to go despite my own uncertainties, as it was there that I met my wife.

I would have no way to prove if my career would have been better if had taken another path, but I can confidently say that my life is fuller and more meaningful as a result of my decision. The point I'm trying to make is to encourage you to embrace the journey you are going to embark on.

Life will take you in many directions. Work hard to make the most of what you have, take chances that will come your way, but don't overthink it. Sometimes you will have to leave your comfort zone, and you will feel uncertain and uncomfortable. That's OK. In my case, those were the times I found myself learning and developing the most.

The world is changing quickly, and there are always new situations that you're not going to be familiar with. No matter what you encounter, have confidence that the skills and knowledge you've acquired will carry you through. And know that your professors will be cheering you on and friends and family will be supporting you along the way.

Topic: 1. _____	
A. Welcome ceremony	
B. Graduation ceremony	
C. Farewell ceremony	
Who are the target audience?	
2. _____	
Introduction	The background and purpose of the speech This is a very 3. _____ moment for you and your entire family. I still vividly remember sitting in your seats 16 years ago as a graduate of the Economics Department.
Body	A "personalized" pattern • Working at Goldman Sachs • Meeting many 4. _____ • Choosing to go to business school in the U.S.
Conclusion	Generalizing life lessons Life is full of challenges and opportunities that require 5. _____, courage, and confidence. You need the skills and knowledge to overcome any obstacles and achieve your goals, with the support of your professors, friends, and family.

Activity Four

Based on the following background, write a topic, a general purpose and a specific purpose with the help of the above public speaking skill.

Here is the background.

Duane Winfield, a student at a large state university, decided to give his first classroom speech on a topic from his personal experience. For the past two years, he had volunteered his time to perform music for patients in mental hospitals, nursing homes, and residences for disabled adults. He had seen how enthusiastically the patients responded to music, even when they remained unmoved by other kinds of stimuli. Duane's experience had given him a better understanding of the benefits of music therapy, and he wanted to share this understanding with his classmates. This gave him a topic and a general purpose.

Topic: _____
General purpose: _____
Specific purpose: _____

Section C Further Listening

Activity One

Listen to five calls and watch each call with their content.

1st call	1. _____	A. Jochen Anderson's schedule complaint and request for a time and title change
2nd call	2. _____	B. Disagreement regarding the speaking time and format for the design seminar
3rd call	3. _____	C. Bryan's confirmation to open the building on Sunday and sharing his contact information
4th call	4. _____	D. Computer courses and seminar details for spreadsheets and accounting software
5th call	5. _____	E. Confirmation of next month's business breakfast meeting and its date

Unit 2
Coding

Activity Two

You will hear two long conversations. Listen and choose the best answer to each question.

Conversation One

1. Where does this conversation take place?
   A. In a hotel.
   B. At a restaurant.
   C. In a travel agency.
   D. In a shop.

2. How does the customer pay the bill?
   A. With a credit card.
   B. With traveler's cheques.
   C. With cash in the local currency.
   D. With cash in U.S. dollars.

3. What do you know about the change?
   A. The waitress gives it to the customer in U.S. dollars.
   B. The waitress gives it to the customer in the local currency.
   C. The customer leaves the change for the waitress as there isn't much left.
   D. There is no change because the customer doesn't pay the bill in cash.

Conversation Two

4. What was the woman doing at lunchtime?
   A. Giving a lecture.
   B. Discussing political science.
   C. Working on a science problem.
   D. Reading 20th-century literature.

5. Which of the following best describes Professor Hawl's relationship with his students?
   A. Professor Hawl is a controversial figure on campus.
   B. Professor Hawl plays an important part in college.
   C. Students admire Professor Hawl for his wonderful lectures.

D. Students are sleeping in Professor Hawl's lecture.

6. How does Professor Hawl feel about his visitors at his lectures?

   A. They make him feel good.

   B. They make no impact on him.

   C. They bore him.

   D. They make him angry.

Activity Three

Listen to a passage about our principles of ecological civilization and fill in each blank within three words.

What Are China's Principles of Ecological Civilization?

The following are the six principles for developing an ecological civilization.

1st principle—Harmonious coexistence between 1. _____ and 2. _____, focusing on environmental conservation, restoration, and protection.

2nd principle—Innovative, coordinated, 3. _____, open, and 4. _____ development that respects environmental limits and addresses problems at their roots.

3rd principle—Improvement of environmental quality and public health, ensuring that the environment benefits 5. _____ and meets their demand for a beautiful 6. _____.

4th principle—A holistic approach to environmental governance that views mountains, rivers, forests, fields, lakes, and grasslands as a biotic 7. _____ and implements comprehensive measures across various domains.

5th principle—The 8. _____ regulations and laws to protect the environment, supported by legal and regulatory innovation and enforcement.

6th principle—Global collaboration in building a global ecological civilization, participating in global environmental 9. _____, influencing the international order, and contributing to environmental protection and 10. _____ development worldwide.

Unit 3

IT Career

Learning Objectives

In this unit, you will:
- learn basic information about the IT career;
- learn to listen to the details of a passage;
- learn to analyze the audience.

Background

IT careers offer diverse opportunities, including roles such as software engineer, network administrator, database administrator, cyber-security analyst, and IT project manager. Professionals in the field are responsible for maintaining and improving technology infrastructure, developing innovative software solutions, ensuring data security, and providing technical support to organizations and individuals.

Section A Listening

Pre-Listening

Work in pairs and discuss the following questions.
1. How many IT career paths do you know? What are they?
2. Why do so many people study information technology?

Activity One

Match each IT expertise with the corresponding job description.

1. IT expertise in cyber-services	A. Implementing network security measures and conducting vulnerability assessments for financial institutions
2. IT expertise in field services	B. Developing software solutions for managing patient records and medical billing in healthcare organizations
3. Knowledge of the healthcare industry	C. Providing on-site technical support and maintenance for industrial equipment in manufacturing plants
4. Knowledge of the finance industry	D. Designing and implementing secure network infrastructure for government agencies and organizations
5. Knowledge of the manufacturing industry	E. Installing and configuring point-of-sale systems and ensuring secure payment processing for retail businesses

Unit 3 IT Career

While-Listening

Text A A Career in Field Services and Cyber-Services

Language Bank

bedrock	['bedrɒk]	n.	牢固根基
leverage	['liːvərɪdʒ]	v.	充分利用（资源、观点等）
infrastructure	['ɪnfrəstrʌktʃə(r)]	n.	（国家或机构的）基础设施，基础建设
validate	['vælɪdeɪt]	v.	证实，验证
military	['mɪlətri]	n.	军队
troubleshoot	['trʌblʃuːt]	v.	故障排解

Activity Two

You will hear a passage about field services. Listen and choose the best answer to each question.

1. What is the bedrock of IT?
   A. Service and support.
   B. Technology.
   C. IT technicians.
   D. Break-fix support.

2. Which is NOT involved in the cloud itself?
   A. Physical infrastructure.
   B. Mobile access.
   C. End users, touch.
   D. IT devices.

3. To get started, which one will you at least want from CompTIA?
   A. Network+.
   B. Security+.
   C. A+ certification.
   D. All of the above.

4. Many tech schools and universities offer all of these EXCEPT _____.
   A. programs that provide a basic background in hardware and software
   B. programs that provide a basic background in networking

C. security certifications

D. certificates from CompTIA

5. What is the main topic of the passage?

A. IT certificates.

B. Basic contents in field services.

C. IT devices.

D. Influence of IT.

Activity Three

You will hear a passage about cyber-services, Listen and decide whether the following statements are true (T) or false (F).

(　　) 1. Cyber-security arguably requires less expertise than field service.

(　　) 2. Every business needs cyber-security or some form of network or data security.

(　　) 3. It is absolutely necessary for the degree to be in the field of security.

(　　) 4. Cyber-security typically requires inside-the-box thinking skills.

(　　) 5. One place to start is with both CompTIA's Security+ certification and software providers.

Text B　IT Expertise with a Specific Industry

Language Bank

expertise	[ˌekspɜːˈtiːz]	n.	专门知识；专门技能
architect	[ˈɑːkɪtekt]	n.	缔造者，创造者
vertical	[ˈvɜːtɪkl]	adj.	垂直的
consultant	[kənˈsʌltənt]	n.	顾问
projection	[prəˈdʒekʃn]	n.	预测；推断
demonstrate	[ˈdemənstreɪt]	v.	展现（才能、品质、感情）

Activity Four

You will hear a passage about IT expertise in a specific industry. Fill in each blank within three words.

Business Consulting / Vertical Industries / Professional Services

One of the best things you can do with IT expertise is combine it with knowledge of a

1. _____ industry. Of course, that requires additional knowledge, experience, or both. But few business workers have 2. _____ of both IT and their industry. The person who comprehends both is invaluable.

A business consultant or technology professional services consultant with IT expertise has 3. _____. Those options could lie within the IT department or within a line of business inside the enterprise. He or she could work as a provider of 4. _____ or as a business consultant independently or as a part of a service organization. There are many channels in the market requiring these skills from solution architects with a(n) 5. _____ (VAR) to a technology consultant or business consultant working as part of an IT channel partner, VAR or even a traditional consulting firm. This is a high-growth, 6. _____ with many routes to service markets as a professional in business and IT combined.

There are several high-growth industries in which IT is increasingly important. These include 7. _____, retail, energy and telecommunication (or evolving areas such as service provider, or SP). For example, healthcare facilities increasingly depend on 8. _____ equipment and data (such as the Internet of Things, or IoT). Any IT expert who also understands the 9. _____ needs of healthcare or a given vertical will be in high demand. Lastly, the topic and technologies within IoT for almost any vertical is an area with huge growth 10. _____. IoT itself will have a very positive impact on careers in each of the topics covered today. We'll expand on this topic more in the future with opinions and projections from industry experts and use cases for you to consider as a potential next step in your IT career.

Activity Five

You will hear a passage about IT management. Listen and decide whether the following statements are true (T) or false (F).

(　　) 1. Anyone can be an IT manager if he has made great efforts before.
(　　) 2. Everyone in an IT career will have to decide whether to continue with a technical focus or shift into a managerial role.
(　　) 3. One place to start is to learn different kinds of programming languages.
(　　) 4. At companies with more than 1,000 employees, it's not unusual for one or two managers to oversee the entire IT function.
(　　) 5. You'll need deep knowledge of not only technology but also business.

Post-Listening

Work in pairs and discuss the following questions.
1. Are you suitable for jobs in the field of IT? Why or why not?
2. Which IT career path do you like most? Why?

Section B Public Speaking

Activity One

Read the passage below and gain some knowledge about audience analysis.

Analyzing Your Audience

Being audience-centered

When you think of your audience, don't imagine some undifferentiated mass of people waiting to hear your message. Instead, think of individuals. Public speaking is the process of speaking to a group of individuals, each with a unique point of view. Good public speakers are audience-centered, which means keeping the audience foremost in mind at every step of speech preparation and presentation. Public speakers should know the primary purpose of speechmaking is not to browbeat the audience or to blow off steam. Rather, it is to gain a desired response from listeners.

Being audience-centered does not involve compromising your beliefs to get a favorable response. Nor does it mean using devious, unethical tactics to achieve your goal. You can remain true to yourself and speak ethically while adapting your message to the goals, values, and attitudes of your audience. To be audience-centered, you need to keep several questions in mind when you work on your speeches:

- To whom am I speaking?
- What do I want them to know, believe, or do as a result of my speech?
- What is the most effective way of composing and presenting my speech to accomplish that aim?

Ways of audience analysis

One of the ways speakers analyze audiences is by looking at demographic traits such as age; gender; religion; sexual orientation; group membership; racial, ethnic, or cultural background; and the like. This is called demographic audience analysis. It consists of two steps: identifying the general demographic features of your audience, and gauging the importance of those features to a particular speaking situation.

Another way is situational audience analysis which usually builds on demographic analysis. It identifies traits of the audience unique to the speaking situation at hand. These traits include the size of the audience, the physical setting, and the disposition of the audience toward the subject, the speaker, and the occasion.

Audience adaptation

Once you have completed the audience analysis, you should have a pretty clear picture of your listeners. But this does not guarantee a successful speech. The key is how well you use what you know in preparing and presenting the speech. This point deserves special attention because it poses one of the hardest tasks facing novice speakers. Most people can identify the major characteristics of their audience, but many have trouble adapting their ideas to the audience. There are two major stages in the process of audience adaptation. The first occurs before the speech, as part of your preparation and rehearsal. Put yourself in their place. Try to hear the speech as they will. Anticipate questions and objections, and try to answer them in advance. The second occurs during the presentation of the speech itself. When you deliver your speech, keep an eye out for audience feedback and adjust your remarks in response.

Activity Two

Answer the following questions according to the passage above.
1. Why should a public speech be audience-centered?
2. What audience analysis skills can you learn from the passage?

Activity Three

Fill in the blanks and complete the outline.

Analyzing Your Audience	
Audience-centered	Being audience-centered does not involve 1. _____ your beliefs to get a favorable response. Nor does it mean using devious, unethical 2. _____ to achieve your goal. You can remain 3. _____ to yourself and speak ethically while adapting your message to the goals, values, and attitudes of your audience.

(Continued)

	Analyzing Your Audience
Audience analysis	Demographic audience analysis is done by looking at 4. _____. Situational audience analysis includes the size of the audience, the physical setting, and the disposition of the audience toward the subject, the speaker, and the occasion.
Audience adaption	There are two major stages in the process of audience adaptation. One is 5. _____, as part of your preparation and rehearsal. And another is 6. _____ of the speech itself.

Activity Four

Prepare an outline with a focus on how to analyze your audience before giving a speech about the IT career. Your speech should address the following questions.

◆ What are the essential skills and training for an IT career?
◆ What are the challenges to pursuing a successful IT career?
◆ What are the job prospects and the evolution of an IT career?

Section C Further Listening

Activity One

Listen to five short recordings and match each speaker to their recordings.

1st speaker 1. _____	A. Considering eco-investment risky and unpredictable due to political factors and varying government approaches
2nd speaker 2. _____	B. Suggesting that nuclear energy may experience a revival as governments realize the long-term energy challenges and limitations of natural sources
3rd speaker 3. _____	C. Discussing wave power as an underrepresented investment option, but predicts slow development and limited returns for small, short-term investors

Unit 3
IT Career

(Continued)

4th speaker 4. _____	D. Believing wind power is a good long-term investment due to its consistent growth
5th speaker 5. _____	E. Advocating for investing in oil, highlighting its continuous growth and the development of environmentally friendly fuels by oil companies

Activity Two

You will hear two long conversations. Listen and choose the best answer to each question.

Conversation One

1. What did the man think about people of the Ice Age?
   A. They lived in caves.
   B. They traveled in groups.
   C. They had an advanced language.
   D. They ate mostly fruit.

2. How did people in the early Ice Age keep warm?
   A. They lived in large groups.
   B. They used sand as insulation.
   C. They kept fires burning constantly.
   D. They faced their homes toward the south.

3. What does the man want the woman to do?
   A. Meet his anthropology teacher.
   B. Lend him her magazine when she's done with it.
   C. Come over to his house after class.
   D. Help him study for an anthropology test.

Conversation Two

4. What are members of the club required to do?
   A. Register when they arrive.
   B. Bring up to three guests.

C. Register their guests.

D. Show membership cards on arrival.

5. What do we know about the lockers according to the conversation?

   A. There is no charge for using the lockers.

   B. Twenty cents should be paid for using the lockers.

   C. Clothes are not advised to be left in the lockers.

   D. It is safer to bring the clothes than leave them in the lockers.

6. How long can members play on the tennis courts?

   A. For 30 minutes only.

   B. For one hour only.

   C. Within the booked time only.

   D. Longer than the booked time.

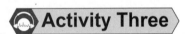 Activity Three

Listen to a passage about Shangqiu and fill in each blank within three words.

Shangqiu

So power came from the ancestors. In the oracle bones, there's a secret place. It has the same name as the dynasty—Shang. The archaeologists now turn to a little town in 1. _____ with a tantalizing name—Shangqiu—the ruins of Shang. Go inside the Ming-Dynasty city. This was built in 2. _____. The previous one long destroyed by 3. _____ was what's underneath it. What's fascinating is that it's still called Shangqiu—the ruins of Shang. So what's this ancestral place of China's first great dynasty? That question has 4. _____ Chinese archaeologists since the first explorations here in the 1930s. But the brown-aged layers here are 5. _____ deep in the Yellow River silt. Recently though, geophysical surveys and tests have detected the 6. _____ of a much earlier city underneath the town. And clues to what it was were in the oracle bones found at Anyang. In the 1930s, a Chinese scholar called Deng Zuobin worked on the brown-aged inscriptions 7. _____ on the oracle bones from the Shang Dynasty. There are thousands upon thousands of them. Through the 1930s, when China was driven by civil war and Japanese 8. _____, he worked transcribing these inscriptions. It could be called self-effacing loyalty to the 9. _____. This transcription of one of the turtle shells with all the inscriptions on them. And it worked on the order of the Shang kings, their 10. _____, their rituals, and their journeys.

Unit 4
Blended Learning

Learning Objectives

In this unit, you will:
- learn about blended learning;
- learn to listen for key information in a passage;
- support your ideas in a public speech.

Background

Nowadays live instruction is not a standardized method of teaching anymore. With the introduction of information technology into classrooms, blended learning is becoming a prominent teaching method which satisfies the needs of different kinds of learners.

Section A Listening

Pre-Listening

Work in pairs and discuss the following questions.

1. What is blended learning?
2. What are the benefits of blended learning?

Activity One

Choose the best answer to each question to see what kind of learner you are.

1. If I have to learn how to do something, I learn best when I _____.
   A. watch someone show me how
   B. hear someone tell me how
   C. try to do it myself

2. When I spell, I verify accuracy by _____.
   A. looking at the word to see if it looks correct
   B. sounding the word out in my head
   C. getting a feeling about the correctness of the spelling

3. When asked to give directions, I _____.
   A. see the actual places in my mind as I say them or prefer to draw them
   B. have no difficulty giving them verbally
   C. have to use my fingers to point or move my body as I give them

4. When I have to remember a list of items, I remember them best if I _____.
   A. write them down

B. repeat them over and over to myself

C. move around and use my fingers to name each item

5. When solving a problem, I _____.

    A. write or draw diagrams to see it

    B. talk myself through it

    C. use and/or move objects to help me think

6. When I am adding numbers, I verify my answer by _____.

    A. looking at the numbers to see if they are correct

    B. counting the numbers in my head or out loud

    C. using my fingers to get a feeling if it is correct

7. When trying to recall names, I remember _____.

    A. faces more easily than names

    B. names more easily than faces

    C. the situation or the meeting more easily than names or faces

8. Before going to sleep at night, I appreciate that _____.

    A. the room is dark

    B. the room is quiet

    C. the bed feels comfortable

While-Listening

Text A Free Online Learning

Language Bank

niche	[niːʃ]	n.	商机；市场定位
massive	['mæsɪv]	adj.	（尺寸、数量、规模）非常大的
integrate	['ɪntɪɡreɪt]	v.	（使）合并，成为一体
trove	[trəʊv]	n.	收藏的东西
compelling	[kəm'pelɪŋ]	adj.	激发兴趣的
sample	['sɑːmpl]	n.	样品；样本

Activity Two

You will hear a passage about free online learning. Listen and choose the best answer to each question.

1. Which of the following forms is NOT mentioned in Coursera?

   A. Discussion forums.

   B. Interactive lessons.

   C. Quizzes.

   D. Lectures.

2. In which case can Khan Academy be a right resource?

   A. Learning how to write the code.

   B. Picking up a new language.

   C. Learning about a topic in short bursts.

   D. Getting to know more about science.

3. What will you choose if you're a user of iPad and iPhone?

   A. EdX.

   B. MIT.

   C. Apple APP.

   D. iTunes U.

4. According to this passage, which is NOT the most useful language to develop interactive websites?

   A. HTML.

   B. Python.

   C. C#.

   D. PHP.

5. What are the more suitable tools for people who want to learn foreign languages?

   A. Livemocha and EdX.

   B. Coursera and Duolingo.

   C. iTunes U and MIT OpenCourseWare.

   D. Duolingo and Livemocha.

Unit 4
Blended Learning

Activity Three

Listen again and decide whether the following statements are true (T) or false (F).

(　　) 1. All these eight websites are free and can be used at home by people with a Web browser and an Internet connection.

(　　) 2. Khan Academy will provide certificates of completion to prove that you passed the class.

(　　) 3. Massachusetts Institute of Technology does well especially in science, computer, and engineering.

(　　) 4. Course materials of EdX come from a number of universities, such as Harvard University and University of Hong Kong.

(　　) 5. You can communicate with native speakers for the purpose of learning a new language in Duolingo.

Text B   The Benefits of Blended Learning

Language Bank

on-demand	[ˌɑndɪˈmɑːnd]	adj.	随选的
corporate	[ˈkɔːpərət]	adj.	集体的；企业的；公司的
aural	[ˈɔːrəl]	adj.	听力的
kinesthetic	[ˌkɪnəsˈθetɪk]	adj.	动觉的
retention	[rɪˈtenʃn]	n.	记忆力
hands-on	[ˌhændzˈɒn]	adj.	亲身实践的
modality	[məʊˈdæləti]	n.	方式
optimal	[ˈɒptɪməl]	adj.	最佳的
scalable	[ˈskeɪləbl]	adj.	可扩增的
modular	[ˈmɒdjələ(r)]	adj.	模块化的

Activity Four

You will hear a passage about blended learning. Listen and choose the best answer to each question.

1. What is blended learning?

   A. The name of a course.

B. An instruction method.

   C. A learning method.

   D. A piece of teaching equipment.

2. What would be the best mode of learning for people who learn visually?

   A. Live instructor-led classrooms.

   B. Hands-on practice from engaging in applied learning projects.

   C. Online self-paced video delivery.

   D. Corporate training.

3. Why does blended learning enable people to control the pace of their learning?

   A. Because there is no live lecture in blended learning.

   B. Because blended learning includes the "human" element of interaction.

   C. Because blended learning utilizes as many learning delivery methods as possible.

   D. Because by studying online, people can study as quickly as they can manage.

4. Which is NOT the reason that blended learning can save money?

   A. Blended learning has the potential to optimize outcomes for individual students.

   B. Blended learning reduces instructor fees, company travel expenses and training materials.

   C. Blended learning enables distance learning at a global scale.

   D. Blended learning can greatly soften the impact training has on daily operations and the employees themselves.

5. All of the following are the benefits of blended learning EXCEPT _____.

   A. blended learning satisfies different kinds of learners

   B. learners can control the pace of their learning

   C. blended learning mixes instructor-led classroom training with online content

   D. blended learning is modular and scalable

Activity Five

Listen again and decide whether the following statements are true (T) or false (F).

(   ) 1. Blended learning is also called "flipped classroom".

(   ) 2. Hands-on practice from engaging in applied learning projects would satisfy social and aural learners.

(　　) 3. For most people, learning cannot be improved by combining different activities alongside more passive study according to studies.

(　　) 4. People learn best when they can control the pace of their learning.

(　　) 5. Blended learning is modular and scalable, especially for small, local enterprises.

Post-Listening

Work in pairs and discuss the following questions.
1. What challenges do educators face when implementing blended learning?
2. How can blended learning be used to accommodate different learning styles?"

Section B Public Speaking

Activity One

Read the passage below and get some knowledge about how to support your ideas.

Supporting Your Ideas

A good speech needs strong supporting materials. Using your supporting materials effectively is essential because audiences crave detail and specifics. Supporting materials make your ideas, arguments, assertions, points, or concepts real and concrete. Sometimes supporting materials are thought of as supports for a bridge. Without these supports, though you might be able to see the beginning and the end, the whole structure would quickly collapse.

In general, there are two basic ways to think about the role of supporting materials.

- They clarify, explain, or provide specifics (and, therefore, understanding) for the audience.
- They provide evidence and, therefore, persuade the audience.

In order to inform and persuade your audience, you need to support your ideas with statistics, examples, and testimony.

- Statistics are a collection of numbers. They are often used to prove facts, describe or draw conclusions about the nature or characteristics of people, objects, or scientific phenomena or highlight trends.
- Examples are also good supporting materials. An example refers to a specific case or an incident used to make an abstract idea concrete. Examples can be brief descriptions or detailed stories. They are often used to clarify, emphasize, and reinforce ideas.

- Testimony refers to quotations or paraphrases of someone who has first-hand experience or expertise in a certain field. A statement from such a person is considered more believable than a statement made by a non-expert.

Activity Two

Answer the following questions according to the passage above.
1. Why are supporting materials essential for effective public speaking?
2. How many basic ways are there to think about the role of supporting materials in general? And what are they?
3. What can be used as the supporting materials?

Activity Three

Read an example of a speech and complete the outline of it.

Building a Museum of Museums on the Web

Hello, everyone. My name is Amit. Eighteen months ago, I had another job at Google, and I pitched this idea of doing something with museums and art to my boss who's actually here, and she allowed me to do it. And it took 18 months. A lot of fun, negotiations and stories, I can tell you, with 17 very interesting museums from nine countries. But I'm going to focus on the demo. There are a lot of stories about why we did this.

I think my personal story is explained very simply on the slide, and it's accessible. And I grew up in India. I had a great education. I'm not complaining, but I didn't have access to a lot of these museums and these artworks. And so when I started traveling and going to these museums, I started learning a lot. And while working at Google, I tried to put this desire to make it more accessible with technology together. So we formed a team, a great team of people, and we started doing this.

I'm going to probably get into the demo and then tell you a couple of the interesting things we've had since launch. So, it's simple: You come to Google Art Project website. You look around at all these museums here. You've got the Uffizi. You've got the MoMA, the Hermitage, the Rijks, the Van Gogh. I'm going to actually get to one of my favorites, the Metropolitan Museum of Art in New York. Two ways of going in. Very simple. Click and, bang, you're in this museum. It doesn't matter where you are, Bombay, Mexico. You move around, and you have fun. You want to navigate around the museum? Open the plan up, and, in one click, jump. You're in there, you want to go to the end of the corridor. Keep going. Have fun. Explore.

Thanks. I haven't come to the best part.

So now I'm in front of one of my favorite paintings, *The Harvesters* by Pieter Bruegel at the Met. I see this plus sign. If the museum has given us the image, you click on it. Now this is one of the images. So this is all of the meta-data information. For those of you who are truly interested in art, you can click this, but I'm going to click this off right now. And this is one of these images that we captured in what we call gigapixel technology. So this image, for example, has close to, I think, around 10 billion pixels. And I get a lot of people asking me: "What do you get for 10 billion pixels?" So I'm going to try and show you what you really get for 10 billion pixels. You can zoom around very simply. You see some fun stuff happening here.

But then you really want to go deep. And so I started playing around, and I found something going on over here. And I was like, "Hold on. That sounds interesting." Went in, and I started noticing that these kids were actually beating something. I did a little research, spoke to a couple of my contacts at the Met, and actually found out that this is a game called squall, which involves beating a goose with a stick on Shrove Tuesday. And apparently it was quite popular. I don't know why they did it, but I learned something about it. Now just to get really deep in, you can really get to the cracks. Now just to give you some perspective, I'm going to zoom out so you really see what you get. Here is where we were, and this is the painting.

The best is yet to come, so in a second. So now let's just quickly jump into the MoMA, again in New York. So another one of my favorites, *The Starry Night*. Now the example I showed you was all about finding details. But what if you want to see brush strokes? And what if you want to see how Van Gogh actually created this masterpiece? You zoom in. You really go in. I'm going to go to one of my favorite parts in this painting, and I'm really going to get to the cracks. This is *The Starry Night*, I think, never seen like this before.

So I think, in conclusion, for me, the main thing is that all the amazing stuff here does not really come from Google. It doesn't, in my opinion, even come from the museums. I probably shouldn't say that. It really comes from these artists. And that's been my humbling experience in this. I mean, I hope in this digital medium that we do justice to their artwork and represent it properly online. And the biggest question I get asked nowadays is, "Did you do this to replicate the experience of going to a museum?" And the answer is no. It's to supplement the experience.

And that's it. Thank you.

Building a Museum of Museums on the Web	
Introduction	The purpose of the speech—doing something with museums and arts

(Continued)

	Building a Museum of Museums on the Web
Body	A "travel"—examples First, you come to Google Art Project website, you look around at all these museums here. You've got the Uffizi, you've got the MoMA, the Hermitage, the Rijks, the 1. _____. Second, I'm in front of one of my favorite paintings, *The Harvesters* by Pieter Bruegel at the Met. I see this plus sign. If the museum has given us the image, you 2. _____ it. Next, just quickly jump into the MoMA, again in New York. So another one of my favorites, 3. _____. Now the example I showed you was all about finding details.
Conclusion	I hope in this 4. _____ that we do justice to their artwork and represent it properly online. And the biggest question I get asked nowadays is, "Did you do this to 5. _____ the experience of going to a museum?" And the answer is no. It's to supplement the experience.

Activity Four

Choose one of the following topics and think over which way you will employ to support your ideas.

◆ How will virtual reality change the world?
◆ How to be smart online learners?
◆ Why is the metaverse important?

Section C Further Listening

Activity One

Listen to five short recordings and match each speaker with their recordings.

1st speaker 1. _____	A. Planning a family holiday and contemplating future options, including potentially working part-time until retirement

Unit 4
Blended Learning

(Continued)

2nd speaker 2. _____	B. Resigning from a job due to boredom
3rd speaker 3. _____	C. Reacting to being accused of misconduct at work
4th speaker 4. _____	D. Discussing the selection process for a position and expressing confidence in the chosen candidate's suitability and flexibility
5th speaker 5. _____	E. Voluntarily leaving a job before potential layoffs to take advantage of a favorable deal and have time to find another job

Activity Two

You will hear two long conversations. Listen and choose the best answer to each question.

Conversation One

1. What does the woman meet the man for?
   A. To make an appointment.
   B. To ask for an interview.
   C. To promote advertisements.
   D. To have a negotiation.

2. Which can best describe the man's reaction to the woman's words?
   A. Impatient but then reluctant.
   B. Indifferent but then interested.
   C. Reluctant but then convinced.
   D. Impatient but then accepted.

3. Which is not true about the service of the woman's company?
   A. Customers can get the payment back if they're not satisfied with the products.
   B. The company will redo the products again and again until the customers are satisfied.
   C. Customers should do exactly according to the contract.
   D. The company charges a proper amount of money.

Conversation Two

4. What's wrong with the woman?
   A. She has a temperature.

B. She suffers from a headache.

C. She has a sore throat.

D. She often feels dizzy.

5. Why does the woman feel ill?

   A. She didn't have enough sleep.

   B. She has caught a bad cold.

   C. She is dying from a serious disease.

   D. She is too nervous to feel at home.

6. What does the man suggest the woman to do?

   A. She should take some medicine and more water.

   B. She should take care of her rest and drink more water.

   C. She should give up her term paper for her health.

   D. She should receive more check-ups.

Activity Three

Listen to a passage about how China is building the digital Silk Road of the 21st century and fill in each blank within three words.

How Is China Building the Digital Silk Road of the 21st Century?

Chinese President Xi Jinping emphasized the importance of core technologies and the need to accelerate advancements in core information technologies. The focus is on building a comprehensive 1. _____ system and coordinating efforts in technology, industry, and policy. Long-term planning and major 2. _____ are emphasized, along with centralized leadership and improved policies in 3. _____, taxation, trade, human resources, and 4. _____ property protection. The aim is to create a fair market environment and oppose monopolies and 5. _____ competition. The integration of basic research and technological innovation is highlighted to drive breakthroughs in 6. _____ technologies.

Regarding global Internet governance, President Xi advocates for a multilateral approach with the 7. _____ of multiple stakeholders such as governments, international organizations, Internet enterprises, tech communities, NGOs, and citizens. 8. _____ governance should be promoted under the framework of the United Nations, while also involving non-state actors. The Belt and Road Initiative presents an opportunity to strengthen 9. _____ with countries along the Belt and Road, especially developing nations, in areas such as Internet infrastructure, the 10. _____ economy, and cyber-security, aiming to establish a digital Silk Road in the 21st century.

Unit 5
IT and Gender Disparity

Learning Objectives

In this unit, you will:
- learn about gender disparity;
- learn to grasp specific information in listening;
- learn to organize the body of a speech.

Background

Digital technology has transformed the way we live and work, providing new opportunities for communication, education, and economic growth. However, women are underrepresented in the technology industry and face barriers to accessing education and training in digital skills. This gender gap in digital technology has significant consequences for economic and social development, as well as for individual well-being and empowerment. Addressing gender disparity in digital technology is therefore an urgent and important challenge for policy-makers, educators, and the technology industry.

Section A Listening

Pre-Listening

Work in pairs and discuss the following questions.

1. What is gender disparity?
2. How does the gender gap in digital technology affect women's access to education and job opportunities?

Activity One

What causes gender disparity, and what strategies can be used to address this issue? Put a "√" in the bracket in front of the influencing factors and strategies, and discuss them with your partners.

Factors that cause gender disparity in the IT industry	( ) 1. Work-life balance
	( ) 2. Lack of representation
	( ) 3. Bias and stereotypes
	( ) 4. Workplace culture
	( ) 5. Training and development
	( ) 6. Supporting women in leadership positions
	( ) 7. Providing family-friendly policies such as flexible work arrangements

(Continued)

Strategies to address gender disparity in the IT industry	( ) 8. Encouraging girls and women to pursue education and careers in IT
	( ) 9. Giving preferential treatment to women over men
	( ) 10. Fostering a culture that values and promotes diversity and inclusion

While-Listening

Text A　Digital Technology and Gender Equality

Language Bank

inequality	[ˌɪnɪˈkwɒləti]	n.	不平等
flexibility	[ˌfleksəˈbɪləti]	n.	灵活性
tackle	[ˈtækl]	v.	解决
transform	[trænsˈfɔːm]	v.	使改观
conservatively	[kənˈsɜːvətɪvli]	adv.	谨慎地，保守地
antenatal	[ˌæntiˈneɪtl]	adj.	产前的
bargain	[ˈbɑːɡən]	v.	谈判
potential	[pəˈtenʃl]	adj.	潜在的

Activity Two

You will hear a passage about the influence of digital technology on gender equality. Listen and choose the best answer to each question.

1. According to the passage, how does digital technology help tackle gender inequality?
   A. By creating more jobs for women than men.
   B. By providing women with more flexible working arrangements.
   C. By eliminating all the challenges that women face.
   D. By enabling women to work in traditionally male-dominated industries.

2. What are the estimated cost savings of providing digital finance compared with physical payments?
   A. 70%–80%.
   B. 80%–90%.

C. 70%–90%.

D. 90%–100%.

3. What has Suncorp done to bring opportunities to women in Australia?

    A. It has provided access to remote healthcare services.

    B. It has offered digital media training.

    C. It has redesigned its contact center through "work at home hubs".

    D. It has provided access to online marketplaces.

4. What aspects of women's abilities can be improved by digital technologies according to the passage?

    A. Digital technologies can only help women earn more money.

    B. Digital technologies can improve women's competitive power.

    C. Digital technologies can help women change others' welfare.

    D. Digital technologies can help women earn money, and improve their health and welfare.

5. How has digital technology helped women in Indonesia gain social status, bargaining positions and influence on village policies?

    A. By providing access to online marketplaces.

    B. By offering remote healthcare services.

    C. By offering digital media training.

    D. By giving them access to bank accounts.

Activity Three

Listen to the passage again to learn about the current status of women in the digital technology field in each region. Choose FIVE answers from the box, and write the correct letters down next to questions 1–5. There are two extra choices in the box.

| A. South Asia | B. India | C. Indonesia | D. Asia Pacific |
| E. North Asia | F. China | G. Southeast Asia | |

1. Women-owned businesses earn 35% of the revenue on the largest online marketplace in the country. _____

2. In this area, approximately 57% of women are economically excluded. _____

3. In this area, approximately 54% of women are economically excluded. _____
4. Women comprise half of the population and contribute 36 percent of the GDP. _____
5. A mobile application used by a Non-Governmental Organization's program helps women become health businesspeople. _____

Text B   Women in the IT Industry

Language Bank

contemporary	[kən'temprəri]	adj.	当代的
constraint	[kən'streınt]	n.	限制
persistence	[pə'sıstəns]	n.	坚持不懈
demonstrate	['demənstreıt]	v.	证明
hybrid	['haıbrıd]	adj.	混合的
endurance	[ın'djʊərəns]	n.	耐力；忍耐力
masculine	['mæskjəlın]	adj.	男子汉的
rhetoric	['retərık]	n.	修辞
privilege	['prıvəlıdʒ]	n.	特权

Activity Four

You will hear a passage about women in the IT industry. Listen and try to decide whether the following statements are true (T) or false (F).

(　　) 1. Despite the growing demand for IT professionals, women are well represented in the UK IT industry.
(　　) 2. This study used original qualitative data from 62 interviews with male and female IT workers and 20 interviews with company and stakeholder representatives.
(　　) 3. This study offers a profound perception to comprehend why women continue to be underrepresented in the field of all kinds of industries.
(　　) 4. The study stressed the need for an informative gendered career boundaries approach.
(　　) 5. This research approach enables a nuanced examination of how agency and context interact to shape career paths.

Activity Five

You will hear the passage again. Listen and fill in each gap within three words.

This research aimed to understand why women are underrepresented in the UK IT industry.

Other views

One optimistic view was that contemporary career forms and characteristics of knowledge work, along with technological progress and 1. _____, would provide women with greater opportunities to participate in the IT industry.

Research content

In this study, the researchers analyzed interviews with male and female IT workers and interviews with company and stakeholder representatives to understand the reasons behind this underrepresentation. And it examines how gender 2. _____ with other personal characteristics, occupational features, organization dynamics, and 3. _____ and institutional factors to create different career constraints for women and men in the IT industry at key stages over their life course.

Research object

The research sheds light on why women are still underrepresented in IT and reveals that the paths of entry previously used by women to access IT careers are 4. _____. It also highlights how gender and motherhood interact with 5. _____ and the hybrid nature of careers to constrain female careers.

Current situation of women

Women and mothers face disadvantages in both 6. _____ and contemporary aspects of their careers, which are impacted by constant change, informality, and the persistence of masculine 7. "_____" norms.

Furthermore, the study argues that the efforts made by IT companies to correct the 8. _____ are little more than half-hearted rhetoric. Gender initiatives in the IT industry tend to favor a small group of women and perpetuate the male-dominated status quo, rather than making meaningful systemic changes.

Research findings

The study finds that the boundaries between organizational and cross-organizational careers are becoming 9. _____ in the IT industry due to the growing emphasis on 10. _____.

Therefore, the study emphasizes the need to form a different idea about female career constraints to a more informative gendered career boundaries approach, which allows for nuanced consideration of the interaction between agency and context in the formation of careers.

Post-Listening

Work in pairs and discuss the following questions.
1. What do you think about gender disparity?
2. What impact does gender diversity have on the performance and success of organizations?

Section B Public Speaking

Activity One

Read the passage below and get some knowledge about organizing the body of a speech.

Organizing the Body of a Speech

Clear organization is vital to speech-making. Listeners demand coherence. They get only one chance to grasp a speaker's ideas, and they have little patience for speakers who ramble aimlessly from one idea to another. A well-organized speech will enhance your credibility and make it easier for the audience to understand your message.

Here is a commonly adopted organizational model, a linear model, which consists of three sections:

Introduction

The purpose of an introduction is to get the attention and interest of the audience at the beginning, tell the audience what your speech is about or the purpose of your speech, and explain briefly how your speech will meet the purpose without mentioning all the details.

Body

The purpose of the body is to cover about 90% of your speech including the detailed arguments that support your thesis statement, in the order of time, space, topic, etc. For informative speeches or in problem-(cause-) solution order for persuasive speeches.

Conclusion

The purpose of the conclusion is to summarize the main points and finish your speech in a confident manner, preferably echoing the introduction.

The process of planning the body of a speech begins when you determine the main points. You should choose them carefully, phrase them precisely, and organize them strategically. Because listeners cannot keep track of a multitude of main points, most speeches should contain no more than two to five. Each should focus on a single idea, be worded clearly, and receive enough emphasis to be clear and convincing.

You can organize the main points in various ways, depending on your topic, purpose, and audience. Chronological order follows a time pattern, whereas spatial order follows a directional pattern. In causal order, the main points are organized according to their cause-effect relationship. Topical order results when you divide your main topic into subtopics. Problem-solution order breaks the body of the speech into two main parts, with the first showing a problem, and the second giving a solution.

Activity Two

Answer the following questions according to the passage above.
1. Why should the speaker make a clear organization?
2. What's the common organizational model?
3. How many ways can be used to order your arguments? What are they?

Activity Three

Read an example of a speech and complete the outline of it.

How Pakistani Women Are Taking the Internet Back

Imagine waking up to a stranger—sometimes multiple strangers—questioning your right to existence for something that you wrote online, waking up to an angry message, scared and worried for your safety. Welcome to the world of cyber-harassment. The kind of harassment that women face in Pakistan is very serious and leads to sometimes deadly outcomes. This kind of harassment keeps women from accessing the Internet—essentially, knowledge. It's a form of oppression.

Pakistan is the sixth most populous country in the world, with 140 million people having access to mobile technologies, and 15 percent Internet penetration. And this number doesn't seem to go down with the rise of new technologies. Pakistan is also the birthplace of the youngest Nobel Peace Prize winner, Malala Yousafzai. But that's just one aspect of Pakistan. Another aspect is where the twisted concept of honor is linked to women and their bodies; where men are allowed to disrespect women and even kill them sometimes in the name of so-called "family honor"; where women are left to die right outside their houses for speaking to a man on a mobile phone, in the name of "family honor." Let me say this very clearly: It's not honor; it's a cold-blooded murder. I come from a very small village in Punjab, Pakistan, where women are not allowed to pursue their higher education. The elders of my extended family didn't allow their women to pursue their higher education or their professional careers. However, unlike the other male guardians of my family, my father was one who really supported my ambitions. To get my law degree, of course, it was really difficult, and [there were] frowns of disapproval. But in the end, I knew it was either me or them, and I chose myself. My family's traditions and expectations for a woman wouldn't allow me to own a mobile phone until I was married. And even when I was married, this tool became a tool for my own surveillance. When I resisted the idea of being surveilled by my ex-husband, he really didn't approve of this and threw me out of his house, along with my six-month-old son, Abdullah. And that was the time when I first asked myself, "Why? Why are women not allowed to enjoy the same equal rights enshrined in our Constitution? While the law states that a woman has the same equal access to the information, why is it always men—brothers, fathers and husbands—who are granting these rights to us, effectively making the law irrelevant?" So I decided to take a step, instead of keeping questioning these patriarchal structures and societal norms. And I founded the Digital Rights Foundation in 2012 to address all the issues and women's experiences in online spaces and cyber-harassment. From lobbying for free and safe Internet to convincing young women that access to the safe Internet is their fundamental, basic, human right, I'm trying to play my part in igniting the spark to address the questions that have bothered me all these years.

With a hope in my heart, and to offer a solution to this menace, I started Pakistan's and the region's first cyber-harassment help line in December 2016—to extend my support to the women who do not know who to turn to when they face serious threats online. I think of the women who do not have the necessary support to deal with the mental trauma when they feel unsafe in online spaces, and they go about their daily activities, thinking that there is a rape threat in their in-box. Safe access to the Internet is access to knowledge, and knowledge is freedom. When I fight for women's digital rights, I'm fighting for equality.

Thank you!

How Pakistani Women Are Taking the Internet Back	
Introduction	The purpose of the speech —When I fight for a woman's digital rights, I am fighting for equality.
Body	**A. Problems:** The kind of harassment that women face in Pakistan is very serious and leads to sometimes deadly outcomes. This kind of harassment keeps women from 1. _____ the Internet—essentially, knowledge. It's a form of 2. _____ .

(Continued)

	How Pakistani Women Are Taking the Internet Back
	B. Solutions: • Instead of keep questioning these 3. _____ structures and societal norms. And I founded the Digital Rights Foundation in 2012 to address all the issues and women's experiences in online spaces and cyber-harassment. • From lobbying for free and safe Internet to 4. _____ young women that access to the safe Internet is their fundamental, basic, human right. • Besides, I started Pakistan's and the region's first cyber-harassment help line in December 2016—to 5. _____ my support to the women who do not know who to turn to when they face serious threats online.
Conclusion	Safe access to the Internet is access to knowledge, and knowledge is freedom. When I fight for women's digital rights, I'm fighting for equality.

Activity Four

Choose one of the following topics and organize the body of the speech with the help of the public speaking skill above.

◆ Gender stereotypes in the IT industry
◆ Women's contributions to the IT industry
◆ Mentoring and empowering women in the IT industry

Section C Further Listening

Activity One

Listen to five short recordings and try to find out what each salesperson is selling.

1st salesperson 1. _____	A. Advertising
2nd salesperson 2. _____	B. Stationery
3rd salesperson 3. _____	C. Home improvements
4th salesperson 4. _____	D. A car
5th salesperson 5. _____	E. Personal organizers

Unit 5
IT and Gender Disparity

Activity Two

You will hear two long conversations. Listen and choose the best answer to each question.

Conversation One

1. How is George feeling now?
   A. Better.
   B. Not too well yet.
   C. Much better.
   D. Even worse.

2. What happened to George?
   A. He was very sick and was taken to the hospital.
   B. He fell and hurt himself badly.
   C. He broke his leg in a traffic accident.
   D. He was working when something suddenly fell onto his head.

3. What is George's trouble now?
   A. His leg is broken and his ribs hurt very much.
   B. He has chest pain and can hardly breathe.
   C. He can hardly remember anything that has happened.
   D. He feels too weak to talk.

Conversation Two

4. What is the man's hobby?
   A. Relaxing.
   B. Watching TV.
   C. Knitting sacks.
   D. Collecting buttons.

5. What does the woman think about the man's hobby?
   A. She thinks it is very helpful.
   B. She thinks it is a waste of time.
   C. She thinks it is very interesting.
   D. She thinks the man can learn a lot from it.

6. What does the phrase "put one's feet up" most probably mean in the conversation?
   A. Have a rest.
   B. Have a good time.
   C. Have a bath.
   D. Have an exercise.

Activity Three

Listen to a passage about the Ming Dynasty and fill in each blank within three words.

For the Ming, China Was the World

The seven voyages between 1405 and 1433 went across the Indian Ocean to the Persian Gulf for the Red Sea and down the coast of East Africa. They brought back new 1. _____, rare foods and plants, exotic 2. _____, even a giraffe which the Chinese identified with the mythical unicorn, an suspicious 3. _____ for the young learned emperor. After the 6th voyage, Yongle Emperor died. And after one more expedition, the new emperor Xuande called the 4. _____.

So why did they stop? The Ming Dynasty at that point was the 5. _____ part on earth, maybe 200 million people. They've been the greatest scientific innovators. They made the great inventions with which the West would want to 6. _____ the world. For some Western commentators, it is believed that the Chinese lack the will to pursue the 7. _____ of the knowledge. But maybe there's something else. Maybe it's about how you use 8. _____. And perhaps the Ming scholar bureaucrats, in the end, realize their interest will be better served pursuing the traditional 9. _____ of Chinese civilization, of achieving harmony between humankind and the cosmos within the borders of China.

The truth is dominating the wider world was not on the Chinese 10. _____. For the Ming, after all, China was the world.

Unit 6
Network Security

Learning Objectives

In this unit, you will:
- learn to use proper words to talk about network security;
- learn to deal with long passages;
- learn to begin and end the speech properly.

Background

How do you know about network security? Though the concept sounds far away from us, when you enter the password of your Internet accounts, you have already been connected to network security. Except for passwords, what are the other aspects of network security? Let us try to find the answer in this unit.

Section A Listening

Pre-Listening

Work in pairs and discuss the following questions.

1. How much do you know about network security?
2. How can we prevent cyber-attacks?

Activity One

Work in small groups to find the best answer to each question.

1. What is the purpose of a firewall in network security?

    A. To protect against viruses and malware.

    B. To control and monitor network traffic.

    C. To encrypt data transmissions.

    D. To provide secure authentication.

2. Which of the following is NOT a recommended practice for creating strong passwords?

    A. Using a combination of uppercase and lowercase letters.

    B. Including personal information like your birthdate or name.

    C. Using a mix of letters, numbers, and special characters.

    D. Creating passwords with a minimum length of 8 characters.

3. What is a common method used by attackers to trick individuals into revealing sensitive information through fraudulent emails or websites?

    A. Phishing.

    B. Malware.

C. Brute force attack.

D. Denial of service attack.

While-Listening

Text A Disregarding of Network Security

Language Bank

pop up	['pɒp ʌp]		突然出现
disregard	[ˌdɪsrɪ'gɑːd]	v.	无视
whopping	['wɒpɪŋ]	adj.	巨大的
haphazardly	[hæp'hæzədli]	adv.	杂乱无章地
status quo	[ˌsteɪtəs 'kwəʊ]	n.	现状
random	['rændəm]	adj.	随意的
neural	['njʊərəl]	adj.	神经的

Activity Two

You will hear a passage about people's disregarding network security. Listen and complete the notes by filling in each blank within three words.

◆ If you want people to pay attention to your security warnings on their computers or mobile devices, you need to make them pop up at 1. _____.

◆ Researchers found these times are less 2. _____ because of "dual task 3. _____", a neural 4. _____ where even simple tasks can't be simultaneously performed without 5. _____ performance loss.

◆ They found that the brain can't handle 6. _____ very well.

◆ And a whopping 87 percent disregarded the messages while they were 7. _____ information, in this case, a(n) 8. _____ code.

◆ Waiting to 9. _____ a warning to when people are not busy doing something else increase their security behavior 10. _____.

Activity Three

Listen again and decide whether the following statements are true (T) or false (F).

( ) 1. A new study finds the status quo of warning messages appearing haphazardly results in up to 90 percent of users disregarding them.

( ) 2. 74 percent of people in the study ignored security messages if they were watching a video.

( ) 3. People pay the most attention to security messages when they pop up in higher dual task times.

( ) 4. Timing security warnings to appear when a person is more likely ready to respond isn't current practice in the software industry.

( ) 5. The experiment showed neural activity was slightly reduced when security messages interrupted a task, as compared with when a user responded to the security message itself.

Text B Security Flaws of the Internet

Language Bank

flaw	[flɔː]	n.	瑕疵
gut	[ɡʌt]	n.	核心
server	['sɜːvə(r)]	n.	服务器
configure	[kən'fɪɡə(r)]	v.	配置
fallout	['fɔːlaʊt]	n.	后果
router	['ruːtə(r)]	n.	路由器
nasty	['nɑːsti]	adj.	严重的

Activity Four

You will hear a passage about the security flaws of the Internet. Listen and decide whether the following statements are true (T) or false (F).

( ) 1. Security experts said the potential for harm could extend much further, to the guts of the Internet and the many devices that connect to it.

( ) 2. Juniper Networks said its products were not affected.

( ) 3. Chuck Mulloy, a spokesman for Intel said so far they had found nothing.

(　　) 4. OpenSSL is built into some of this hardware like home routers and printers.

(　　) 5. Security researchers say that there has been an increase in black market sales of sensitive data, like passwords.

Activity Five

Listen again and choose the best answer to each question.

1. Which kind of products Cisco makes were NOT affected?
   A. Some kinds of phones that connect to the Internet.
   B. Servers that help people conduct online meetings.
   C. Devices used for office communications.
   D. Its online servers.

2. What does OpenSSL do?
   A. It helps save information on the Internet.
   B. It helps protect information on the Internet.
   C. It helps encrypt information on the Internet.
   D. It helps steal information on the Internet.

3. Which one is NOT the reason why the problem caused by the Heartbleed bug is so nasty?
   A. OpenSSL is built into some of this hardware like home routers and printers connected to the Internet.
   B. The web—with sites like Facebook and Google—is the most visible part of the Internet.
   C. OpenSSL goes far beyond just websites.
   D. OpenSSL is implemented in email protocols and all kinds of embedded devices.

4. Why was most of the equipment made by Cisco and Juniper unaffected?
   A. They did not use OpenSSL for their encryption.
   B. The companies don't make home routers.
   C. They have protection systems.
   D. They are immune from the bug.

5. According to Mr. Kurtz, if users want to be absolutely secure, what are they advised to do?
   A. Stop using OpenSSL.
   B. Change a new home router.
   C. Check with their home router manufacturers to upgrade their devices.
   D. Upgrade their software.

Post-Listening

Work in pairs and discuss the following questions.

1. Will you ignore the security messages when they pop up on web pages? Why or why not?
2. Have you ever been hacked? Can you give some ideas on how to avoid being hacked?

Section B Public Speaking

Activity One

Read the passage below and get some knowledge about beginning and ending a speech.

Beginning and Ending a Speech

Introduction

First impressions are important. A poor beginning may distract or alienate listeners so much that the speaker can never fully recover. A good introduction, you will find, is an excellent confidence booster. In most speech situations, the introduction has four objectives:

- Get the attention and interest of your audience;
- Reveal the topic of your speech;
- Establish your credibility and goodwill;
- Preview the body of the speech.

Gaining attention and interest can be done in several ways. You can show the importance of your topic, especially as it relates to your audience. You can startle or question your audience or arouse their curiosity. You can begin with a quotation or a story. Be sure to state the topic of your speech clearly in your introduction so the audience knows where the speech is going. Establishing credibility means that you tell the audience why you are qualified to speak on the topic at hand. Establishing goodwill may be necessary if your point of view is unpopular. Previewing the body of the speech helps the audience listen effectively and provides a smooth lead-in to the body of the speech.

Conclusion

Your final impression will probably linger in your listeners' minds. Thus you need to craft your conclusion with as much care as your introduction. No matter what kind of speech you are giving, the conclusion has two major functions:

- To let the audience know you are ending the speech;
- To reinforce the audience's understanding of, or commitment to, the central idea.

You can accomplish this by summarizing the speech, ending with a quotation, making a dramatic statement, or referring to the introduction. Sometimes you may want to combine two or more of these techniques. Be creative in devising a vivid, forceful conclusion.

Activity Two

Answer the following questions according to the passage above.
1. What are the four objectives of an introduction in most speech situations?
2. What are the two major functions of a conclusion?

Activity Three

Read an example of a speech and complete the outline of it.

Don't Like Clickbait? Don't Click

So recently, some white guys and some black women swapped Twitter avatars, or pictures online. They didn't change their content. They kept tweeting the same as usual, but suddenly, the white guys noticed they were getting called the n-word all the time and they were getting the worst kind of online abuse, whereas the black women all of a sudden noticed things got a lot more pleasant for them.

Now, if you're my five-year-old, your Internet consists mostly of puppies and fairies and occasionally fairies riding puppies. That's a thing. Google it. But the rest of us know that the Internet can be a really ugly place. I'm not talking about the kind of colorful debates that I think are healthy for our democracy. I'm talking about nasty personal attacks. Maybe it's happened to you, but it's at least twice as likely to happen, and be worse, if you're a woman, a person of color, or gay, or more than one at the same time. In fact, just as I was writing this talk, I found a Twitter account called @SallyKohnSucks. The bio says that I'm a "man-hater and a bull dyke and the only thing I've ever accomplished with my career is spreading my perverse sexuality." Which, incidentally, is only a third correct. I mean, lies!

But seriously, we all say we hate this. The question is whether you're willing to make a personal sacrifice to change it. I don't mean giving up the Internet. I mean changing the way you click, because clicking is a public act. It's no longer the case that a few powerful elites control all the media and the rest of us are just passive receivers. Increasingly, we're all the media. I used to think, oh, okay, I get dressed up, I put on a lot of makeup, and I go on television, I talk about the news. That is a public act of making media. And then I go home and I browse the web and I'm reading Twitter, and that's a private act of consuming media. I mean, of course it is. I'm in my pajamas. Wrong. Everything we blog, everything we Tweet, and everything we click is a public act of making media. We are the new editors. We decide what gets attention based on what we give our attention to. That's how the media works now. There are all these hidden algorithms that decide what you see more of and what we all see more of based on what you click on, and that in turn shapes our whole culture.

Over three out of five Americans think we have a major incivility problem in our country right now, but I'm going to guess that at least three out of five Americans are clicking on the same insult-oriented, rumor-mongering trash that feeds the nastiest impulses in our society. In an increasingly noisy media landscape, the incentive is to make more noise to be heard, and that tyranny of the loud encourages the tyranny of the nasty.

It does not have to be that way. It does not. We can change the incentive. For starters, there are two things we can all do. First, don't just stand by the sidelines when you see someone getting hurt. If someone is being abused online, do something. Be a hero. This is your chance. Speak up. Speak out. Be a good person. Drown out the negative with the positive. And second, we've got to stop clicking on the lowest-common-denominator, bottom-feeding linkbait. If you don't like the 24/7 all Kardashian all the time programming, you've got to stop clicking on the stories about Kim Kardashian's sideboob. I know you do it. You too, apparently. I mean, really, the same example: if you don't like politicians calling each other names, stop clicking on the stories about what one guy in one party called the other guy in the other party. Clicking on a train wreck just pours gasoline on it. It makes it worse, the fire spreads. Our whole culture gets burned.

If what gets the most clicks wins, then we have to start shaping the world we want with our clicks, because clicking is a public act. So click responsibly.

Thank you.

Don't Like Clickbait? Don't Click	
Introduction	**Beginning:** Get attention and establish the credibility The purpose of the speech—changing the way you click, click responsibly
	A. Problems: We have a major 1. _____ problem in our country right now, but I'm going to guess that at least three out of five Americans are clicking on the same insult-oriented, rumor-mongering trash that feeds the nastiest 2. _____ in our society.

Unit 6
Network Security

(Continued)

	Don't Like Clickbait? Don't Click
Body	**B. Solution:** • First, don't just stand by the 3. _____ when you see someone getting hurt. If someone is being 4. _____ online, do something. • Second, we've got to stop clicking on the 5. _____, bottom-feeding linkbait.
Conclusion	**Reinforce the audience's understanding of the central idea** If what gets the most clicks wins, then we have to start 6. _____ the world we want with our clicks, because clicking is a public act. So click responsibly.

Activity Four

Choose one of the following topics and prepare an introduction and a conclusion with the help of the public speaking skill above.

◆ Network security and privacy in the age of big data
◆ Data storage centralization
◆ Cyber-insurance

Section C Further Listening

Activity One

Listen to five short recordings and try to find out what each speaker is talking about.

1st speaker	1. _____	A. Confirming arrival time
2nd speaker	2. _____	B. Requesting help in retrieving project plans from Lucy's office
3rd speaker	3. _____	C. Inquiring about obtaining an overdraft facility and seeking guidance on setting up an online banking account
4th speaker	4. _____	D. Expressing frustration over not receiving a response after applying for a secretary position

(Continued)

| 5th speaker 5. _____ | E. Informing someone about the decision to start work on a specific date and the need for an additional site manager |

Activity Two

You will hear two long conversations. Listen and choose the best answer to each question.

Conversation One

1. What does Annie think of White's course?
   A. Very good.
   B. Interesting.
   C. Too specialized.
   D. Too general.

2. Which course does Professor White teach in the university?
   A. Logic.
   B. Writing.
   C. History.
   D. Mathematics.

3. What can we learn from the dialogue?
   A. The man chose Professor White's course once.
   B. The woman is in favor of Professor White.
   C. Professor White's course is welcomed by the students.
   D. The man won't choose Professor White's course anymore.

Conversation Two

4. In which kind of conversation style do people take turns to give opinions?
   A. The bowling style.
   B. The rugby style.
   C. The basketball style.
   D. The NBA style.

5. Which of the following does NOT often use the rugby style of conversation?
   A. Southern Europe.
   B. Northern Europe.
   C. Russia.
   D. Latin America.

6. What do Americans mean by saying "T like table?" in the example?
   A. To make sure that the letter is "T" instead of "D".
   B. To tell the physician he needs a table.
   C. To indicate the physician is like a table.
   D. To make fun of the physician.

Activity Three

Listen to a passage about Chinese education and fill in each blank within three words.

How Can the Chinese Education System Be Improved?

Since the 18th CPC National Congress in 2012, remarkable progress has been made in education reform, but many more things need to be done as this is a(n) 1. _____ campaign involving many factors and facets. Last year, the 2. _____ authorities issued the "Opinions on Deeper Reform of the Education System", requiring that we follow the established practices and principles of educational development and the way students grow to create a vibrant, 3. _____, and more open education system which is conducive to high-quality education.

Our drive to modernize education should be 4. _____, maintain the nature of education as a public undertaking, ensure equal access to education as the basic national policy, and promote 5. _____ in reforming the education system.

We should make education available to every 6. _____ throughout their life and make studying a habit and a lifestyle choice so that people can study whenever and wherever they want to. We should guarantee 7. _____ access to education, trying to make good education available to everyone regardless of gender, 8. _____ and ethnicity, and whether they are rich or poor, or from an urban or rural area. We should make education adaptable to each individual's needs, enabling students with different temperaments, interests, and 9. _____ to receive an education suitable to their growth. We should build a more open and flexible education system to offer more choices to students to expand their path for growth and clear the ladder to academic excellence, career advancement, and upward 10. _____.

Unit 7

Cyber-Attack and Cyber-Bullying

Learning Objectives

In this unit, you will:
- learn the information about cyber-attack;
- learn to grasp the key words of cyber-attack and cyber-bullying;
- learn to outline a speech.

Background

Cyber-bullying and cyber-security incidents and breaches are two common problems in the modern, Internet-driven world. While the two have similarities in that they both involve malicious actors online, the motives are quite different. However, the points of connection between these two topics are worth exploring.

Section A Listening

Pre-Listening

Work in pairs and discuss the following questions.

1. What is cyber-attack?
2. Can you give any examples of the advantages and disadvantages of the Internet?

Activity One

Work in pairs to talk about the meaning of the comics below.

Unit 7　Cyber-Attack and Cyber-Bullying

While-Listening

Text A　Cyber-Crime

Language Bank

spotty	['spɒti]	adj.	发疹的
notoriety	[ˌnəʊtə'raɪəti]	n.	恶名
tricky	['trɪki]	adj.	棘手的
installation	[ˌɪnstə'leɪʃn]	n.	安装
staggering	['stæɡərɪŋ]	adj.	令人震惊的
savvy	['sævi]	n.	实际知识；见识

Activity Two

You will hear a speech about cyber-crime. Listen and choose the best answer to each question.

1. Which one is NOT right about cyber-criminals in the following statements?
   A. They are wonderfully professional and organized.
   B. They have the product adverts.
   C. They work in the basement.
   D. You can buy the services from them.

2. What can we get about the Black Hole Exploit Pack?
   A. It's the market leader in malware distribution.
   B. Half of the malware distribution is completed by it.
   C. It will attack your computer with video.
   D. It will attack its own website.

3. According to the speech, what do we need to think of when we adopt new applications and mobile devices?
   A. Whether they are good enough or not.
   B. The number of the people who are using them.
   C. How much we are spending on them.
   D. Personal privacy and security.

4. Why are the legal issues in the area of cyber-criminals challenging?

   A. Legal issues in this area are complicated.

   B. Cyber-criminals steal lots of money.

   C. The Internet is borderless.

   D. Most laws are only implemented within a country.

5. What can we do to prevent malware from working?

   A. To see some astonishing stories in the news.

   B. To know that malware is doing incredible and terrifying, scary things

   C. To do some basics, such as updating your computer and getting a secure password.

   D. To ask the specialists for help.

Activity Three

Listen again and decide whether the following statements are true (T) or false (F).

(   ) 1. The cyber-criminals could get lots of products and services including a testing platform.

(   ) 2. More crimes are packed with business intelligence reporting dashboards because cyber-criminals want to manage the distribution of their malicious code.

(   ) 3. When you install something, look at the settings and make sure they are suitable for your computers or phones.

(   ) 4. Despite difficulties, the cyber-criminals who steal millions of dollars have been arrested.

(   ) 5. The majority of malware works because they are too strong.

Text B Online Attack

Language Bank

hacktivist	[ˈhæktɪvɪst]	n.	黑客活动分子
plausible	[ˈplɔːzəbl]	adj.	貌似可信的
encrypt	[ɪnˈkrɪpt]	v.	将……译成密码
totalitarian	[təʊˌtælə'teəriən]	adj.	极权主义的
dissident	[ˈdɪsɪdənt]	n.	意见不同的人
trustworthy	[ˈtrʌstwɜːði]	adj.	可靠的
Security Socket Layer (SSL)			加密套接字协议层(一种加密的通讯协定)

Unit 7
Cyber-Attack and Cyber-Bullying

Activity Four

You will hear a passage about the types of online attacks. Listen and fill in each blank within three words.

Online attacks could be classified based on the 1. _____.

We actually have several cases of 2. _____. These guys make their fortunes online, but they make it through the 3. _____ of using things like 4. _____ to steal money from our bank accounts while we do online banking, or with key loggers to collect 5. _____ while we are doing online shopping from a(n) 6. _____. So it's more likely to become the victim of a(n) 7. _____ than here in the real world. In the future, the 8. _____ will happen online.

The second major group of attackers is not motivated by money. They're motivated by something else—motivated by 9. _____, motivated by 10. _____, and motivated by the laughs.

Activity Five

You will continue to listen to the passage. Decide whether the following statements are true (T) or false (F).

( ) 1. There are three main attackers: criminals for the money, hacktivists for the protest, and the Western government.
( ) 2. The dissidents in countries such as Iran like Gmail, because it is more reliable.
( ) 3. Only totalitarian governments would use attack tools against their own citizens.
( ) 4. State Trojan could infect your computer and enable users to watch all your communication, to listen to your online discussions, to collect your passwords.
( ) 5. Privacy is not up for discussion. This is a question of privacy versus security.

Post-Listening

Work in pairs and discuss the following questions.

1. In your opinion, which type of online attack is the worst?
2. How can we deal with online attacks?

Section B Public Speaking

Activity One

Read the passage below and get some knowledge about outlining a speech.

Outlining a Speech

An outline is like a blueprint for your speech. It allows you to see the full scope and content of your speech at a glance. By outlining, you can judge whether each part of the speech is fully developed, whether you have adequate supporting materials for your main points, and whether the main points are properly balanced. An outline helps you make sure that related items are together, that ideas flow from one to another, and that the structure of your speech will "stand up"—and not collapse.

By outlining, you make sure that related ideas are together, that your thoughts flow from one to another, and that the structure of your speech is coherent. You will probably use two kinds of outlines for your speeches—the detailed preparation outline and the brief speaking outline.

In the preparation outline, you state your specific purpose and central idea; label the introduction, body, and conclusion; and designate transitions, internal summaries, and internal previews. You should identify main points, subpoints, and sub-subpoints by a consistent pattern of symbolization and indentation. Your instructor may require a bibliography with your preparation outline.

The speaking outline should contain key words or phrases to jog your memory, as well as essential statistics and quotations. Make sure your speaking outline is legible, follows the same visual framework as your preparation outline, and includes cues for delivering the speech.

Activity Two

Answer the following questions according to the passage above.

1. What's the definition of an outline?
2. What's the purpose of an outline?
3. How many kinds of outlines can you use for speeches?

Unit 7
Cyber-Attack and Cyber-Bullying

 **Activity Three**

Read an example of a speech and complete the outline of it.

Better Cyber-Security Starts with Honesty and Accountability

Today, I'm going to talk about a shameful topic. This has happened to many of us, and it's embarrassing, but if we don't talk about it, nothing will ever change. It's about being hacked. Some of us have clicked on a phishing link and downloaded a computer virus. Some of us have had our identities stolen. And those of us who are software developers might have written insecure code with security bugs in it without realizing it. As a cyber-security expert, I have worked with countless companies to improve their cyber-security. Cyber-security experts like me have advised companies on good cyber-security practices, monitoring tools and proper user behaviors. But I actually see a much bigger problem that no tool can fix: the shame associated with the mistakes that we make.

We like to think of ourselves as competent and tech savvy, and when we make these mistakes that can have a really bad impact on us and our companies—anything from a simple annoyance, to taking a lot of time to fix, to costing us and our employers a lot of money. Despite billions of dollars that companies spend on cyber-security, practitioners like me see the same problems over and over again. Let me give you some examples.

The 2015 hack of Ukrainian utilities that disconnected power for 225,000 customers and took months to restore back to full operations started with a phishing link. By the way, 225,000 customers are a lot more than 225,000 people. Customers can be anything from an apartment building to an industrial facility to a shopping mall. The 2017 data breach of Equifax that exposed personally identifiable information of 140 million people and may ultimately cost Equifax something on the order of 1.4 billion dollars, which was caused by an exploitation of a well-known vulnerability in the company's customer consumer complaint portal.

In a digitally interconnected world, cyber risks are literally everywhere. For years, my colleagues and I have been talking about this elusive notion of cyber-security culture. Cyber-security culture is when everybody in the organization believes that cyber-security is their job, knows what to do and what not to do and does the right thing. Unfortunately, I can't tell you which companies do this well, because by doing so, I would put a juicy target on their backs for ambitious attackers. But what I can do is to make cyber-security less mysterious, bring it out into the open and talk about it. There should be no mystery or secrecy within an organization. When something is invisible and it's working, we don't know that it's there until it's not there. Kind of like toilet paper. When the COVID-19 pandemic began, what has been there all of a sudden became super important because we couldn't find it anywhere. Cyber-security is just like that: When it's working, we don't know, and we don't care. But when it's not working, it can be really, really bad.

Cyber-security is a journey. It's not a destination, and we need to keep working on it. I would love for us to celebrate cyber-security people like the heroes that they are. If we think about it, they are firefighters, emergency room doctors and nurses, law enforcement, risk executives and business strategists all in the same persona. And they help us protect our modern life that we like so much. They protect our identities, our inventions, our intellectual property, our electric grid, medical devices, connected cars and myriad other things. And I'd like to be on that team. So let's agree that this thing is with us to stay, let's create a safe environment to learn from our mistakes, and let's commit to making things better.

	Better Cyber-Security Starts with Honesty and Accountability
Introduction	The purpose of the speech—keep working on cyber-security
Body	A. Subpoint 1: After being hacked, a much bigger problem that no tool can fix is the shame 1. _____ with the mistakes that we make. • Example 1: The 2015 hack of Ukrainian 2. _____ that disconnected power for 225,000 customers and took months to restore back to full operations started with a phishing link. • Example 2: The 2017 data breach of Equifax that 3. _____ personally identifiable information of 140 million people and may ultimately cost Equifax something on the order of 1.4 billion dollars. B. Subpoint 2: In a digitally 4. _____ world, cyber risks are literally everywhere.
Conclusion	Cyber-security is a journey. It's not a(n) 5. _____, and we need to keep working on it. Let's create a safe environment to learn from our mistakes, and let's commit to making things better.

Activity Four

Choose one of the following topics and make an outline of your speech with the help of the public speaking skill above.

◆ How to protect your mental well-being on social media
◆ How to argue on the Internet without losing your mind
◆ How to deal with online shaming

Unit 7
Cyber-Attack and Cyber-Bullying

Section C Further Listening

Activity One

Listen to a conversation between a student and the university work-study coordinator. Fill in each blank within three words.

1. Who is Mr. Terry?
   Answer: Mr. Terry is the person Allison needs to talk to about a(n) _____ job for the work-study program.

2. What is the work-study program?
   Answer: The work-study program is a program offered by the _____ to meet one of Allison's financial aid requirements.

3. Why did Allison come to see Mr. Terry early?
   Answer: Allison came to see Mr. Terry early because she had a problem with her housing situation and needed to straighten it out at _____ with the housing advisor.

4. What is the time constraint for Allison's meeting with Mr. Terry?
   Answer: Mr. Terry has a workshop in _____ minutes, so he won't have much time to meet with Allison.

5. How many job options does the school offer in different departments?
   Answer: The school offers a(n) _____ of job options in many different departments.

6. How many jobs are currently available for students?
   Answer: There are only _____ jobs remaining.

7. What does Allison find appealing among the available positions?
   Answer: Allison finds the campus bookstore job and the _____ interesting.

8. What is the difference between the campus bookstore job and the computer lab assistant position?
   Answer: The campus bookstore job is relatively routine and predictable, while the computer lab assistant position requires a lot of _____ know-how and can be quite demanding and stressful.

9. What experience does Allison have that could help her in the computer lab assistant position?
   Answer: Allison was a(n) _____ during her high school years and knows most

computer software programs inside and out, so she'd be comfortable handling tech questions or issues.

10. What is the next step for Allison after choosing the computer lab assistant position?
    Answer: Allison needs to set up an interview with the _____ supervisor.

Activity Two

You will listen to a talk. Complete the outline below by filling in each blank within three words.

Aztec

I. General History

The Aztec empire existed between the 1. _____ century.

The 2. _____ of Aztec was in the center of the modern Mexico City.

II. Food

The staple food of the Aztec empire was 3. _____ which has been domesticated for thousands of years, and spread to the rest of the world from Mexico.

4. _____ are also part of the Aztec diet.

III. Clothing

The clothing of the Aztec was diverse based on different 5. _____.

Aztec clothes were generally made of imported cotton or a yate fiber.

The Aztecs were able to create beautiful colors using a lot of 6. _____.

IV. Education

Girls were instructed about cooking, caring for a family, 7. _____ and ways to economically run the home.

Boys, however, learned trades, fighting skills and 8. _____ skills.

V. Religion

The Aztecs went to temples to 9. _____ and send their tribute.

The tribute included not only agricultural produce but also 10. _____ goods.

Unit 7
Cyber-Attack and Cyber-Bullying

 Activity Three

Listen to a passage about the compass and fill in each blank within three words.

Compass

The compass is a device showing geographic directions by using the Earth's magnetic field. It enabled 1. _____ and exploration to develop on a worldwide scale.

Early in the Warring States Period, while mining ores and 2. _____ copper and iron, Chinese people chanced upon a(n) 3. _____ magnetite that attracted iron and pointed fixedly north. Referred to as a "south-pointer", the 4. _____ compass is made of magnetic lodestone, and the plate is bronze. The circular center represents Heaven, and the square plate represents 5. _____.

Chinese characters on the plate denote the 6. _____ main directions of north, northeast, east, etc. This type of compass has been scientifically 7. _____ and found to work tolerably well. The earliest record of the use of the compass in navigation was in the Song Dynasty.

Without the invention of the compass, many historic 8. _____ such as Zheng He's seven voyages to the Western Seas, Christopher Columbus' discovery of America, the voyage to India by Vasco da Gama, and Ferdinand Magellan's round-the-world voyage would have been 9. _____.

The compass vehicle was an ancient Chinese vehicle equipped with many 10. _____ and a wooden figure that always pointed south no matter which direction the vehicle went. It's an earlier and more primitive form of compass.

Unit 8
Data Theft

Learning Objectives

In this unit, you will:

- learn how to protect personal information;
- learn to guess the answer according to the key words;
- learn to use language in a public speech.

Background

The digitization of information has made it easier for us to access to our information. But meanwhile, it has also brought about the problem of data theft. The stolen data could include passwords, software code or algorithms, and proprietary processes or technologies. Data theft is considered a serious security and privacy breach, with potentially severe consequences for individuals and organizations.

Section A Listening

Pre-Listening

Work in pairs and discuss the following questions.

1. What would you do if your information were let out, such as date of birth, ID number, and telephone number?
2. Do you think any individual or organization who leaks personal privacy unintentionally should assume legal liability?

Activity One

Work in small groups to discuss and choose the best answer to each question.

1. What is data security?
   A. The practice of protecting digital information from unauthorized access, corruption, or theft throughout its entire lifecycle.
   B. The practice of ensuring that data is only used for its intended purpose and by authorized parties.
   C. The practice of encrypting data to make it unreadable to anyone who does not have the key.
   D. The practice of deleting data after it is no longer needed.

2. What are some common causes of data breaches?
   A. Cyber-criminal activities, insider threats, and human error.
   B. Natural disasters, power outages, and hardware failures.
   C. Software bugs, network congestion, and outdated protocols.
   D. All of the above.

3. What are some examples of data security tools and technologies?

   A. Encryption, data masking, and redaction.

   B. Firewalls, antivirus software, and VPNs.

   C. Password managers, biometric authentication, and multi-factor authentication.

   D. All of the above.

4. What are some benefits of having a strong data security awareness program?

   A. Reducing the risk of data breaches and complying with regulatory requirements.

   B. Enhancing the trustworthiness and reputation of the organization.

   C. Improving the efficiency and productivity of the workforce.

   D. All of the above.

While-Listening

Text A XcodeGhost

Language Bank

malicious	[mə'lıʃəs]	adj.	恶毒的
embed	[ɪm'bed]	v.	把……牢牢地嵌入
legitimate	[lɪ'dʒɪtɪmət]	adj.	合法的
stringent	['strɪndʒənt]	adj.	（法律、规章、标准等）严格的
counterfeit	['kaʊntəfɪt]	adj.	伪造的；仿造的
malware	['mælweə(r)]	n.	恶意软件

Activity Two

You will hear a passage about XcodeGhost. Listen and choose the best answer to each question.

1. How many malicious software programs have been found in the App Store up to now?

   A. Four.

   B. Five.

   C. Six.

   D. Seven.

2. How did the hackers embed the malicious software in these Apple apps?

   A. By threatening the founder of legitimate programs to work for them.

   B. By convincing developers to utilize the counterfeit version of iOS and Mac apps.

   C. By persuading developers to use the pirated-illegally versions of Apple's software.

   D. By bribing the senior officials of cyber-security firms.

3. According to Apple's spokeswoman, what did Apple do to cope with hacker attacks?

   A. Removed the apps created with counterfeit software from the App Store.

   B. Worked with developers to rebuild apps by using the proper versions of Xcode.

   C. Cooperated with police to arrest these hackers.

   D. Both A and B.

4. Why is the malware attack regarded as "a pretty big deal"?

   A. Because the App Store couldn't find a way out of the dilemma.

   B. Because it could be hard to defend against if other attackers copy that approach.

   C. Because the hackers would do anything evil to threaten our society.

   D. Not mentioned.

5. According to the researchers, which one does not belong to the infected apps?

   A. Didi Kuaidi.

   B. A music app from NetEase.

   C. WeChat.

   D. A video app from Tencent.

Activity Three

Listen again and decide whether the following statements are true (T) or false (F).

(　　) 1. XcodeGhost is a malicious program which was embedded in all the legitimate apps of cyber-security firms.

(　　) 2. There had been such reports about malicious software making its way past Apple's approval process before this attack.

(　　) 3. iPhone and iPad users could take some steps to check whether their devices were infected.

(　　) 4. There have not been data theft or other harms in Palo Alto Networks up to now.

(　　) 5. Apple hasn't estimated how many apps had been tainted with XcodeGhost.

Text B Data Theft of Yahoo

Language Bank

desensitize	[dɪˈsensətaɪz]	v.	使不敏感
infraction	[ɪnˈfrækʃn]	n.	违反
unnerving	[ˌʌnˈnɜːvɪŋ]	adj.	使人紧张不安的
belie	[bɪˈlaɪ]	v.	掩饰
looting	[luːtɪŋ]	n.	抢劫
encryption	[ɪnˈkrɪpʃn]	n.	数据加密
jeopardy	[ˈdʒepədi]	n.	（被告处于被判罪或受处罚的）危险境地
repercussion	[riːpəˈkʌʃn]	n.	（某事所产生的）持续不良影响

Activity Four

You will hear a passage about data theft of Yahoo. Listen and choose the best answer to each question.

1. Which of the following is NOT a question raised by the sheer scale of infraction?

    A. Customers' worry about the company's management.

    B. Public disclosure and issues over the future.

    C. People's desperation about data security on the Internet.

    D. Whether Yahoo took enough care of its customers' personal data.

2. How much does Yahoo charge about its sale to Verizon?

    A. $50 million.

    B. $5 billion.

    C. $4.8 billion.

    D. $48 million.

3. What makes the Yahoo case striking and unnerving?

    A. It is the first case that discloses a large number of users' information.

    B. It went apparently undetected for two years.

    C. Yahoo shirks its responsibility after data leakage.

    D. Not mentioned.

4. What do the outdated and vulnerable encryption systems suggest?

   A. The insufficient funds of Yahoo.

   B. An uncomfortably lax security culture.

   C. A lack of technical personnel.

   D. The low credibility of Yahoo.

5. Why did consumers worry that the data breach may lead to their accounts at other sites being compromised?

   A. Because the attackers are excellent at stealing information.

   B. Because their passwords of other accounts were also stolen in this data breach.

   C. Because many consumers use the same passwords on multiple platforms.

   D. Because they forgot the passwords of their accounts at other sites.

Activity Five

Listen again and decide whether the following statements are true (T) or false (F).

(　) 1. Although no high-value information was extracted, Yahoo should not shirk its responsibility for its failure to notice the cyber-incursion.

(　) 2. The massive stolen data was sold for $180 on the so-called dark web and was reported by *Vice Motherboard*.

(　) 3. Yahoo adopted positive measures immediately in the wake of the discovery of the leakage, which is satisfactory for customers.

(　) 4. Yahoo became aware of the scale of the problem at once when a breach was being investigated.

(　) 5. The deal between Yahoo and Verizon will be affected by the disclosures about the Yahoo case.

Post-Listening

Work in pairs and discuss the following questions.

1. What do you think of data theft?
2. What can we do to prevent hacker attacks?

Section B Public Speaking

Read the passage below and get some knowledge about using language.

Using Language

Good speakers have respect for language and how it works. As a speaker, you should be aware of the meanings of words and know how to use language accurately, clearly, vividly, and appropriately. Words have two kinds of meanings—denotative meaning and connotative meaning. Denotative meaning is precise, literal, and objective. Connotative meaning is more variable, figurative, and subjective. It includes all the feelings, associations, and emotions that a word touches off in different people.

Using language accurately is vital to a speaker. Never use a word unless you are sure of its meaning. If you are not sure, look up the word in a dictionary. As you prepare your speeches, ask yourself constantly, "What do I really want to say? What do I really mean?" Choose words that are precise and accurate.

Using language clearly allows listeners to grasp your meaning immediately. You can ensure this by using words that are known to the average person and require no specialized background, by choosing concrete words in preference to more abstract ones, and by eliminating verbal clutter.

Using language vividly helps bring your speech to life. One way to make your language more vivid is through imagery, which you can develop by using concrete language, simile, and metaphor. Another way to make your speeches vivid is by exploiting the rhythm of language with parallelism, repetition, alliteration, and antithesis.

Using language appropriately means adapting to the particular occasion, audience, and topic at hand. It also means developing your own language style instead of trying to copy someone else's.

The subject of inclusive language can be complex, but a number of inclusive usages have become so widely accepted that no aspiring speaker can afford to ignore them. They include avoiding the generic "he", dropping the use of "man" when referring to both men and women, refraining from stereotyping jobs and social roles by gender, and using names that groups use to identify themselves.

Activity Two

Answer the following questions according to the passage above.

1. What are the two kinds of meanings that words have?
2. What are some ways to make language vivid in a speech?
3. What are some inclusive usages that an aspiring speaker should be aware of?

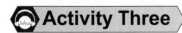

Read an example of a speech and complete the outline of it.

How YouTube Thinks About Copyright

So, if you're in the audience today, or maybe you're watching this talk in some other time or place, you are a participant in the digital rights ecosystem. Whether you're an artist, a technologist, a lawyer or a fan, the handling of copyright directly impacts your life. Rights management is no longer simply a question of ownership, it's a complex web of relationships and a critical part of our cultural landscape. YouTube cares deeply about the rights of content owners, but in order to give them choices about what they can do with copies, mashups and more, we need to first identify when copyrighted material is uploaded to our site.

Let's look at a specific video so you can see how it works. Two years ago, recording artist Chris Brown released the official video of his single "Forever". A fan saw it on TV, recorded it with her camera phone, and uploaded it to YouTube. Because Sony Music had registered Chris Brown's video in our Content ID system, within seconds of attempting to upload the video, the copy was detected, giving Sony the choice of what to do next.

But how do we know that the user's video was a copy? Well, it starts with content owners delivering assets into our database, along with a usage policy that tells us what to do when we find a match. We compare each upload against all of the reference files in our database. This heat map is going to show you how the brain of the system works. Here we can see the original reference file being compared to the user generated content. The system compares every moment of one to the other to see if there's a match. This means that we can identify a match even if the copy used is just a portion of the original file, plays it in slow motion and has degraded audio and video quality. And we do this every time that a video is uploaded to YouTube. And that's over 20 hours of video every minute. When we find a match, we apply the policy that the rights owner has set down.

And the scale and the speed of this system is truly breathtaking. We're not just talking about a few videos, we're talking about over 100 years of video every day, between new uploads and the legacy scans we regularly do across all of the content on the site. When we compare those hundred years of video, we're comparing it against millions of reference files in our database. It would be like 36,000 people staring at 36,000 monitors each and every day, without so much as a coffee break.

Now, what do we do when we find a match? Well, most rights owners, instead of blocking, will allow the copy to be published. And then they benefit through the exposure, advertising and linked sales. Remember Chris Brown's video "Forever"? Well, it had its day in the sun and then it dropped off the charts, and that looked like the end of the story, but sometime last year, a young couple got married. This is their wedding video. You may have seen it.

What's amazing about this is, if the processional of the wedding was this much fun, can you imagine how much fun the reception must have been? I mean, who are these people? I totally want to go to that wedding.

So their little wedding video went on to get over 40 million views. And instead of Sony blocking, they allowed the upload to occur. And they put advertising against it and linked from it to iTunes. And the song, 18 months old, went back to number four on the iTunes charts. So Sony is generating revenue from both of these. And Jill and Kevin, the happy couple, they came back from their honeymoon and found that their video had gone crazy viral. And they've ended up on a bunch of talk shows, and they've used it as an opportunity to make a difference. The video's inspired over 26,000 dollars in donations to end domestic violence. The "JK Wedding Entrance Dance" became so popular that NBC parodied it on the season finale of *The Office*, which just goes to show, it's truly an ecosystem of culture. Because it's not just amateurs borrowing from big studios, but sometimes big studios borrowing back.

By empowering choice, we can create a culture of opportunity. And all it took to change things around was to allow for choice through rights identification. So why has no one ever solved this problem before? It's because it's a big problem, and it's complicated and messy. It's not uncommon for a single video to have multiple rights owners. There are musical labels. There are multiple music publishers. And each of these can vary by country. There are lots of cases where we have more than one work mashed together. So we have to manage many claims to the same video.

YouTube's content ID system addresses all of these cases. But the system only works through the participation of rights owners. If you have content that others are uploading to YouTube, you should register in the Content ID system, and then you'll have the choice about how your content is used. And think carefully about the policies that you attach to that content. By simply blocking all reuse, you'll miss out on new art forms, new audiences, new distribution channels and new revenue streams.

But it's not just about dollars and impressions. Just look at all the joy that was spread through progressive rights management and new technology. And I think we can all agree that joy is definitely an idea worth spreading. Thank you.

	How YouTube Thinks About Copyright
Introduction	The purpose of the speech —How does YouTube think about copyright and what does it do
Body	• First: To identify when copyrighted material is 1. _____ to our site. • Second: How do we know that the user's video was a copy? It starts with content owners 2. _____ assets into our database, along with a usage policy that tells us what to do when we find a match. • Third: What do we do when we find a match? Well, most rights owners, instead of 3. _____, will allow the copy to be published. • Fourth: By 4. _____ choice, we can create a culture of opportunity. And all it took to change things around was to allow for choice through rights identification.
Conclusion	YouTube's content ID system addresses all of these cases. But the system only works through the participation of rights owners. If you have content that others are uploading to YouTube, you should 5. _____ in the Content ID system, and then you'll have the choice about how your content is used.

Activity Four

Choose one of the following topics and write an outline of a public speech. The outline should include an introduction, the main body and a conclusion, and you should list your viewpoints in each part with the help of the public speaking skill above.

◆ On protecting the digital data

◆ In defense of online anonymity

◆ About data theft and hacking

Section C Further Listening

Activity One

Listen to a conversation between a student and his ancient history professor. Fill in each blank within three words.

1: What is the significance of attending the play in New York?
Answer: Attending the play in New York provides the students with the opportunity to see a production of Aeschylus' *The Persians* performed by the National Theater of Greece, which is the earliest surviving _____.

2: Who is Aeschylus and when did he live?
Answer: Aeschylus was an ancient Greek playwright who lived in the _____ century BC.

3. What makes *The Persians* play unusual?
Answer: *The Persians* is considered unusual because it talks about _____ that were occurring around the time it was written, specifically the Persian wars.

4. Are there any other Greek plays that discuss contemporary events?
Answer: The conversation mentions that *The Persians* is the _____ Greek play that discusses current events from that time. Other plays on similar topics may have existed but have been lost.

5. Why does the student express concerns about not enjoying the play?
Answer: The student is concerned about not understanding the language in which the play is performed, which might hinder their ability to fully _____ the experience.

6. What does the professor suggest the student do to obtain a copy of the syllabus?
Answer: The professor advises the student to get a copy of the syllabus from a classmate since the student _____ his/her own copy.

7. What is the professor's response to the student's concerns?
Answer: The professor reassures the student that they will study the play beforehand, making them familiar with it. They also mention that subtitles, known as "_____", will be projected across the top of the stage.

8. What does the student compare the use of "super titles" to?

   Answer: The student compares the use of "super titles" to subtitles in _____.

9. What language was the student's previous opera in?

   Answer: _____.

10. Did the student enjoy the opera despite the language barrier?

    Answer: Yes, the student admits that although it was _____ at first, not understanding the words, they eventually enjoyed the opera and gained a lot from the experience.

Activity Two

You will hear an introduction to a physics course. Complete the outline and fill in each blank within three words.

Physics 101 Syllabus

I. Course Information

Course name: Physics 101

Meeting schedule: Two days a week

Lab session: Three-hour lab on 1. _____

II. Attendance Policy

Attendance is highly encouraged and considered important.

Missing more than 2. _____ class sessions will result in reporting your name to the Dean of Students.

Inexcusable absences may lead to a failing mark in the course.

A(n) 3. _____ lab session counts as two missed class sessions.

III. Preparing for Absences

Inform the instructor in advance if you know you will be absent.

Obtain any assignments, homework readings, 4. _____, or tests for the missed session.

IV. Makeup Exams

Missed quizzes or tests can be made up during the instructor's office hours (4:00 p.m. to 5:00 p.m. Monday through Friday).

Makeup exams must be scheduled within 5. _____ days of the missed exam.

V. Grading Policy

Grades will be based on four tests, several quizzes, and six theme papers.

Formal rules of 6. _____ must be followed.

Spelling errors deduct 10 marks, and inadequate punctuation can cost up to 15 marks.

Late submissions will not be 7. _____ .

VI. Required Readings

Students must read all assigned materials.

Quizzes on reading assignments will be given to ensure 8. _____ the reading.

VII. Office Hours

Instructors' office is located on the 9. _____ floor of the building in front of the current classroom.

Office hours coincide with 10. _____ days (2:00 p.m. to 4:00 p.m.).

Activity Three

Listen to a passage about the first Chinese writing and fill in each blank within three words.

Discovering the First Chinese Writing

The modern discovery of the Shang Dynasty is one of the most exciting stories in the world of archaeology. And it began by chance in one of those storehouses of age-old Chinese wisdom, a traditional 1. _____ , where beliefs and practices go back into prehistory and come down to us today. And the 2. _____ to the mystery of the Shang, unbelievably, were found inside a package of over the counter meds. The story goes like this. In 3. _____ , a Chinese scholar called Wang Yirong, was the chancellor of the Imperial Academy in Beijing, a great scholar, and a(n) 4. _____ of ancient bronzes. He was interested in the 5. _____ Chinese writing system. He fell ill with malaria and a local pharmacy, just like this one delivered a series of 6. _____ which include dragon bones. These were animal bones just like those used today, which you ground up and boil, try to 7. _____ the fever. When he opened the packet, to his amazement, this was what he saw. Some of the bones were inscribed with what he could see were 8. _____ of the old writing that he knew from inscriptions on his bronzes. And eventually these dragon bones were 9. _____ to a little place in the lower valley of the Yellow River, a country town called Anyang. At Anyang, Chinese archaeologists made their greatest discovery, 10. _____ of the last Shang kings, with mass human sacrifice and crucially written texts on oracle bones.

Unit 9

Internet Addiction

Learning Objectives

In this unit, you will:

- learn expressions of describing the bad effects of Internet addiction;
- learn to listen for main ideas;
- learn to deliver the speech.

Background

With the development of information technology, the Internet has become an indispensable part of our lives. But this has brought about the issue of Internet addiction. Though it is not yet an officially recognized mental disorder, many cases have caught our sight. What is Internet addiction and how to deal with it? Let us try to find the answer in this unit.

Section A Listening

Pre-Listening

Work in pairs and discuss the following questions.

1. What is Internet addiction?
2. What are the symptoms of Internet addiction?

Activity One

Here are the top eight social media sites and apps worldwide. Work in small groups to discuss the following questions.

1. Can you name some of the most popular social media sites and apps in China currently?
2. Which one is your favorite and why?

Facebook   YouTube

Instagram   Facebook Messenger

QQ   WeChat

Unit 9
Internet Addiction

TikTok

Sina Weibo

While-Listening

Text A TikTok Addiction

Language Bank

flop	[flɒp]	v.	重重地落下（或掉下）
scroll	[skrəʊl]	v.	滚动
full-blown	[ˌfʊl ˈbləʊn]	adj.	充分发展的
correlation	[ˌkɒrəˈleɪʃn]	n.	相互关系
extraversion	[ˌekstrəˈvɜːʃn]	n.	（性格）外向性
dopamine	[ˈdəʊpəmiːn]	n.	多巴胺
distracted	[dɪˈstræktɪd]	adj.	注意力分散的
reflexively	[rɪˈfleksɪvli]	adv.	本能反应地

Activity Two

You will listen to a passage about TikTok addiction. Listen and decide whether the following statements are true (T) or false (F).

(   ) 1. Of TikTok's 1 billion monthly worldwide users, about 30% of them have a risk of developing an addiction to the app.

(   ) 2. Even if a person is addicted to a social networking site, he or she can successfully control the participation in it.

(   ) 3. There does not exist a correlation between the risk of developing a TikTok addiction and gender.

(   ) 4. People want to keep scrolling through TikTok because of the effect of dopamine.

(   ) 5. Putting a time cap on the app through your phone's setting will not help reduce the time you spend on TikTok.

 **Activity Three**

Listen again and complete the answers to the questions within three words in each blank.

◆ What is the percentage of people who are at risk of becoming addicted to TikTok?
Of TikTok's 1 billion monthly worldwide users, 6.4% are 1. _____ developing an addiction to the app, while 25.4 % are at 2. _____.

◆ What are the signs of addiction to social media platforms?
The user becomes 3. _____, irritable, anxious, or exhibits strong 4. _____ when deprived of access to the social networking site and the user's attempts to control participation in it are unsuccessful.

◆ How is TikTok addiction correlated to gender and previous mental issues?
TikTok users "at-risk" of addiction tended to score higher in terms of 5. _____ and extraversion, while female TikTok users were also more likely to be "at-risk" compared with 6. _____.

◆ Why is TikTok so addictive?
When you're scrolling sometimes you see something delightful and it 7. _____, and you get a little dopamine hit in the 8. _____, in the pleasure center of the brain, which makes you want to keep scrolling.

◆ How to deal with TikTok addiction?
First, 9. _____ you spend on the app or delete it.
Second, 10. _____ from it.
Third, speak to a trusted person.

Text B   Screen Addiction

Language Bank

documentary	[ˌdɒkjuˈmentri]	n.	纪录片
junkie	[ˈdʒʌŋki]	n.	<俚>吸毒者
clinical	[ˈklɪnɪkl]	adj.	临床的
afflict	[əˈflɪkt]	v.	使受痛苦
adept	[əˈdept]	adj.	擅长于……的
therapy	[ˈθerəpi]	n.	治疗
pediatrics	[ˌpiːdiˈætrɪks]	n.	儿科
soothe	[suːð]	v.	安慰；缓和
infringe	[ɪnˈfrɪndʒ]	v.	侵犯；违反
epidemic	[ˌepɪˈdemɪk]	n.	流行病

Unit 9
Internet Addiction

Activity Four

You will hear a passage related to screen addiction. Listen and decide whether the following statements are true (T) or false (F).

( ) 1. Chinese doctors say the therapy has been proven effective.
( ) 2. Internet addiction has been considered a clinical diagnosis.
( ) 3. According to a Kaiser Family Foundation study in 2010, older children and teenagers spend more than 8 hours per day with a variety of different media.
( ) 4. According to a Kaiser Family Foundation study in 2010, television remains the dominant medium.
( ) 5. The academy stated two-thirds of those questioned in the Kaiser study said their parents had some rules about how much time the youngsters spent with media.

Activity Five

You will continue to listen to the passage and answer the following questions by filling in each blank within three words.

1. Why are parents grateful for electronics?
   Answer: Parents are grateful for ways to calm disruptive children and keep them from interrupting their own _____.

2. Why does the pediatrics academy maintain that children should not be exposed to any electronic media before age two?
   Answer: Because a child's brain develops rapidly during these first years, and young children learn best by _____, not screens.

3. How so do teenagers who spend a lot of time playing violent video games or watching violent shows on television behave, according to a study in the *Journal of Youth and Adolescence*?
   Answer: They have been found to be _____ and more likely to fight with their peers and argue with their teachers.

4. On average, how many texts do teenagers send a night after they get into bed according to an earlier Pew study?
   Answer: An earlier Pew study found that teenagers send an average of _____ texts a night after they get into bed.

5. According to Ms. Hatch, why do children begin to feel more lonely and depressed?
   Answer: As children have more of their communication through electronic media, and less of it _____, they begin to feel more lonely and depressed.

Post-Listening

Work in pairs and discuss the following questions.
1. What are the effects of Internet addiction?
2. How can we avoid Internet addiction?

Section B Public Speaking

Activity One

Read the passage below and get some knowledge about delivering a speech.

Delivering a Speech

Delivering a speech is the process of presenting a message verbally and nonverbally to an audience. It's not just about what you say, but how you say it. Delivering a speech can be a challenging and rewarding experience. Whether you are speaking for a class, a work presentation, or a special occasion, you want to make a good impression and convey your message effectively. Here are ten tips for delivering a speech that engages your audience:

- Practice and prepare. The more familiar you are with your speech, the more confident you will be. Rehearse your speech several times, preferably in front of a mirror or a friend who can give you feedback. You can also record yourself and watch your performance to identify areas for improvement.

- Watch for feedback and adapt to it. Pay attention to the verbal and nonverbal cues of your audience, such as their facial expressions, body language, and comments. If they seem bored, confused, or distracted, you may need to adjust your speech accordingly. For example, you can use humor, stories, or questions to regain their attention and interest.

- Let your personality come through. Be yourself and show your passion for the topic. Your audience will be more engaged if they can relate to you as a person and not just a speaker. Use a natural and conversational tone that reflects your personality and emotions.

- Use humor, tell stories, and use effective language. These are some of the techniques that can make your speech more interesting and memorable for your audience. Humor can lighten the mood and break the ice, stories can illustrate your points and connect with your listeners, and effective language can convey your message clearly and persuasively.
- Get rid of any distractions. Before you start your speech, make sure you have nothing in your mouth or hands that might distract you or your audience. Also, check that your microphone, slides, or other equipment are working properly.
- Stand or sit up straight. Your posture affects your voice quality and your confidence level. Avoid slouching, twisting, or leaning on anything that might make you look unprofessional or uncomfortable. Instead, stand or sit up straight with your weight balanced and your shoulders relaxed.
- Make eye contact. Eye contact is one of the most important aspects of nonverbal communication. It shows that you are interested in your audience and that you care about their feedback. It also helps you establish rapport and credibility with them. Try to look at different parts of the room and avoid staring at one spot or person for too long.
- Use gestures. Gestures can enhance your speech by adding emphasis, expression, and clarity to your words. They can also help you release some nervous energy and appear more confident. However, avoid overusing or repeating gestures that might become distracting or annoying for your audience. Use gestures that are natural, appropriate, and relevant to your speech.
- Vary your voice. Your voice is one of the most powerful tools you have as a speaker. It can convey meaning, emotion, and attitude to your audience. To avoid sounding monotonous or boring, vary your voice by changing the pitch, volume, rate, and tone of your speech according to the situation and the message you want to deliver.
- Keep it short. Unless you have a specific time limit for your speech, it is usually better to keep it short and concise than to drag it on for too long. Your audience will appreciate it if you respect their time and attention span. A good rule of thumb is to aim for 10 minutes or less for an informal speech.

Activity Two

Answer the following questions according to the passage above.
1. What is the definition of delivering a speech?
2. Why is delivering a speech important?

3. What are the ten tips for delivering a speech?

Activity Three

Read a passage about some common mistakes to avoid when delivering a speech and complete the outline of it.

Some Common Mistakes to Avoid When Delivering a Speech

Neglecting to prepare. Preparation is key to a successful speech. Without it, you may stumble over your words, forget your main points, or lose your confidence. To avoid this, practice your speech several times, preferably in front of a mirror or a friend who can give you feedback. You can also record yourself and watch your performance to identify areas for improvement.

Using filler words. Filler words are words or sounds that you use to fill the gaps in your speech, such as "um", "uh", "like", "you know", etc. They can make you sound unsure, unprofessional, or unprepared. To avoid this, pause instead of using filler words, and focus on breathing and speaking clearly.

Talking too fast. Talking too fast can make you sound nervous, anxious, or impatient. It can also make it hard for your audience to follow your message or catch your main points. To avoid this, slow down your speech and use pauses for emphasis and clarity. You can also practice with a timer and adjust your speed accordingly.

Talking too softly. Talking too softly can make you sound timid, weak, or uninterested. It can also make it hard for your audience to hear you or pay attention to you. To avoid this, project your voice and use a microphone if necessary. You can also practice in a large room or outdoors and ask someone to listen from a distance and give you feedback on your volume.

Forgetting to make eye contact. Eye contact is one of the most important aspects of nonverbal communication. It shows that you are interested in your audience and that you care about their feedback. It also helps you establish rapport and credibility with them. To avoid this, look at different parts of the room and avoid staring at one spot or person for too long. You can also practice with a friend and ask them to monitor your eye contact and give you feedback.

Using distracting mannerisms. Distracting mannerisms are gestures or movements that you make unconsciously or habitually that may distract your audience from your message or annoy them. Examples include clenching or wringing your hands, pacing back and forth, keeping your hands in pockets, jingling change or keys, twisting your ring, gripping the lectern, licking your lips, adjusting your hair or clothing, fidgeting with a pen, bobbing your head, placing your arms behind your back, and touching your face. To avoid this, record yourself speaking and watch the playback to identify and eliminate any distracting mannerisms. You can also practice with a friend and ask them to point out any distracting mannerisms that you make.

Having low energy. Having low energy can make you sound bored, tired, or unenthusiastic. It can also make your audience feel the same way. To avoid this, show some passion and excitement for your topic and your audience. You can also use gestures, facial expressions, vocal variety, and humor to add some energy and interest to your speech.

Sharing too much information. Sharing too much information can make you sound unfocused, rambling, or boring. It can also overwhelm your audience with details that they may not remember or care about. To avoid this, limit your speech to a few key points that support your main message. Use examples, stories, or anecdotes to illustrate your points rather than facts or statistics. Also use transitions and signposts to help your audience follow the structure and flow of your speech.

\multicolumn{2}{c}{Some Common Mistakes to Avoid When Delivering a Speech}	
Neglecting to prepare	• Impact of insufficient preparation • Importance of practice and feedback • Utilizing 1. _____, friends, and self-recording for improvement
Using filler word	• Definition and examples of filler words • Negative impression caused by filler words • Emphasizing 2. _____ and clear speech
Talking too fast	• Consequences of speaking too quickly • Techniques for slowing down speech • Practicing with a timer and adjusting speed
Talking too softly	• Effects of speaking too softly • Importance of projecting voice • Utilizing 3. _____ and feedback for volume control
Forgetting to make eye contact	• Significance of eye contact in nonverbal communication • Establishing rapport and credibility • Techniques for maintaining proper eye contact
Using distracting mannerisms	• Definition and examples of distracting mannerisms • Impact of distracting mannerisms on the audience • Identifying and 4. _____ distracting mannerisms through self-recording and feedback

(Continued)

	Some Common Mistakes to Avoid When Delivering a Speech
Having low energy	• Negative impression caused by low energy • Ways to showcase passion and enthusiasm • Utilizing gestures, facial expressions, vocal variety, and humor
Sharing too much information	• Consequences of overwhelming the audience with excessive information • Focusing on a few 5. _____ points that support the main message • Using examples, stories, and transitions to enhance understanding

Activity Four

Choose one of the following topics and think about how to deliver a public speech related to self-development with the help of the public speaking skill above.

◆ How to overcome the fear of public speaking
◆ How to boost your confidence
◆ How to set and achieve your goals

Section C Further Listening

Activity One

Listen to a conversation between a student and a dining services director. Fill in each blank within three words.

1. Why did the student's parents buy them a 235-meal plan?
   Answer: The student's parents thought it would be convenient for the student to not worry about _____ during their first year of college.

2. Is it common for first-year students to have meal plans?
   Answer: _____.

3. Can the student choose the 95 meal plan for next year?
   Answer: No, the 95 meal plan is only available for _____ and 4th-year students.

4. Why can only juniors and seniors choose the 95 meal plan?
   Answer: Juniors and seniors are expected to have other _____ options, such as off-campus housing or joining clubs that provide meals.

5. What is the smallest meal plan available to the student for next year?
   Answer: The smallest meal plan available to the student for next year is the _____ meal plan.

6. Are juniors and seniors required to purchase meal plans?
   Answer: _____.

7. Can the student carry over his/her unused meals from this year's plan to next year?
   Answer: _____.

8. Can the student get a refund for his/her unused meals?
   Answer: _____.

9. How many people can the student invite to eat with him/her on his/her meal plan?
   Answer: The student can invite up to _____ people to eat with him/her on his/her meal plan.

10. Should the student talk to the dean about the meal plan policy?
    Answer: The student could talk to the dean about the meal plan policy, but the student doesn't have time at the moment due to _____. The student may consider it in the future.

Activity Two

You will hear a talk about the history of chess. Complete the summary below by filling in each blank within three words.

The History of Chess

Chess originated in either Afghanistan or 1. _____ around the year 600 AD. However, the game might even be 2. _____ years old.

There is an international agreement on the 3. _____ but some variations exist, e.g., in Japan and 4. _____.

The variety played in Europe and America came from Iran and was established in Italy and Spain around the year 1,000 AD. The Vikings took it to Scandinavia and it had reached Central

Europe by 5. _____ AD using the present day rules.

The 6. _____ used today in championships originated in the 19th century and were named after an English chess champion.

The first official championship took place in 1866 in London. To avoid running overtime, they used a(n) 7. _____.

The winner was from Bohemia—in effect the first 8. _____. He held the record until 1894 when he was beaten by a German-born American who was then beaten by a Cuban named Capablanca. Some people rank Capablanca among the 9. _____ who ever lived.

Also in this league was Bobby Fischer—the first 10. _____ to become World Chess Champion.

Activity Three

Listen to a passage about ancient Chinese science and technology and fill in each blank within three words.

Ancient Chinese Science and Technology

For more than a millennium, from the Qin Dynasty to the early period of the Ming Dynasty, Chinese science and technology contributed greatly to the progress of human civilization.

Ancient China has a well-developed agricultural system along with advanced 1. _____. It also boasted an independent tradition in 2. _____ and some advanced botanical knowledge.

China's Four Great Inventions, namely, the 3. _____, gunpowder, paper-making and printing, not only changed the world but also accelerated the evolution of world 4. _____. China further contributed to the world with its rich 5. _____ of silk and porcelain.

The world's most detailed and earliest astronomical 6. _____ were kept by the Chinese. They are the first to take note of such astronomical phenomena as comets, 7. _____ and new stars, producing the most advanced astronomical 8. _____ apparatus of the time.

China played a(n) 9. _____ role in metallurgy. Cast iron was produced in China in as early as the 10. _____ BC, while it was produced sporadically in Europe in the 14th century.

Unit 10

Digital Economy

Learning Objectives

In this unit, you will:

- learn about the digital economy;
- learn to guess main ideas according to questions or your own knowledge;
- learn to use visual aids.

Background

Information technology has influenced our lives so greatly that our way of living in almost all respects has been changed. The business has also been changed by information technology, and the product spawned by the combination of business and IT is called the digital economy. How does the digital economy change business? Let us try to find the answer in this unit.

Section A Listening

Pre-Listening

Work in pairs and discuss the following questions.

1. What are the differences between the digital economy and the Internet economy?
2. Why is the digital economy important?

Activity One

Work in pairs and look at the following comics about the digital economy. Then talk about the meaning of the comics.

Unit 10 Digital Economy

While-Listening

Text A An Introduction to the Digital Economy

Language Bank

real-time	[ˌriːəl ˈtaɪm]	adj.	实时的
novelty	[ˈnɒvlti]	n.	新奇；新奇的事物
tablet	[ˈtæblət]	n.	平板电脑
proximity	[prɒkˈsɪməti]	n.	接近；临近
authentication	[ɔːˌθentɪˈkeɪʃn]	n.	验证；认证
irrigation	[ˌɪrɪˈɡeɪʃn]	n.	灌溉

Activity Two

You will hear an introduction to the digital economy. Fill in each blank within three words.

I. Definition

"Digital economy" refers to the use of 1. _____ to create or adapt, market or consume 2. _____.

II. The Three Things About the Digital Economy

◆ Infrastructure

Businesses have software, hardware and other 3. _____, plus specialist human talent.

◆ E-business

Computer applications, online tools and digital platforms help carry out 4. _____.

◆ E-commerce

A familiar concept, e-commerce means the sale of goods and services online.

III. 5. _____ of the Digital Economy

◆ Information

Consumers have more information to 6. _____ about goods and services.

◆ Proximity

Direct 7. _____ channels enable customers to resolve queries and issues with a manufacturer or service provider more quickly.

◆ 8. _____

With goods and services available for consumers anytime and anywhere, companies can enter more markets.

◆ Security

Digital technology, like strong authentication of 9. _____, makes transactions more secure.

IV. Conclusion

10. _____ sectors have also been transformed by digital economy.

Activity Three

Listen again and decide whether the following statements are true (T) or false (F).

(   ) 1. Personal finance has not been influenced by technology so far.
(   ) 2. People's connection to the global environment is limited by time and space.
(   ) 3. There are three components that distinguish the digital economy from the regular economy.
(   ) 4. The digital economy is bound to become more important.
(   ) 5. Technological innovation contributes little to the development of agriculture.

Text B The Role of Digital Economy in Transforming Business

Language Bank

breakneck	[ˈbreɪknek]	adj.	高速而危险的
backbone	[ˈbækbəʊn]	n.	支柱
undermine	[ˌʌndəˈmaɪn]	v.	逐渐削弱
enablement	[ɪˈneɪblmənt]	n.	可行
cusp	[kʌsp]	n.	分界线
melding	[meldɪŋ]	n.	融合

Activity Four

You will hear a passage related to the role of the digital economy in transforming business. Listen and choose the best answer to each question.

1. The following choices are all the ways to achieve digital transformation EXCEPT _____.
   A. using the latest technology to do what you have already done

B. replacing manual processes with digital ones

C. replacing outdated digital technology with upgraded digital technology

D. connecting people, organizations, and machines

2. What has highlighted the need for digital enablement of the workforce?

   A. The 2020 pandemic.

   B. The emergence of global enterprises.

   C. Digital technology.

   D. Hyperconnectivity.

3. The following choices are all experiences that customers desire while engaging with brands EXCEPT _____.

   A. direct experience

   B. contextual experience

   C. personalized experience

   D. convenient experience

4. What can the Internet of Things do?

   A. Analyze data without sensors on physical objects.

   B. Connect the digital and physical worlds.

   C. Predict the future.

   D. Manage business for people.

5. What is the passage mainly about?

   A. The advantage of the digital economy.

   B. The fundamental areas of the digital economy.

   C. The digital transformation in the digital economy.

   D. The definition of global economy.

Activity Five

Listen again and complete the answers to the questions by filling in each blank within three words.

1. What is digital transformation?

   Answer: Digital transformation refers to the adoption of _____ to transform services or businesses.

2. What does hyperconnectivity, the backbone of the digital economy mean?
   Answer: Hyperconnectivity means growing _____ of people, organizations, and machines that results from the _____, _____, and the Internet of things.
3. What should organizations do to make people experience the same level of connectivity experienced in the physical office no matter where they work?
   Answer: Organizations need to manage a(n) _____ of talent and enable next-generation _____ that prove to be effective, even when distributed across various places and time zones.
4. How do customers want to interact with businesses in the digital economy?
   Answer: In the digital economy, all customers—business-to-business as well as business-to-consumer alike—want to interact with businesses _____ they want and in a fashion that is _____ for them.
5. What are the functions of the data generated by IoT solutions?
   Answer: This data can transform businesses, revealing hidden _____ that can help you make more informed decisions and _____ quickly.

Post-Listening

Work in pairs and discuss the following questions.
1. To what extent has the digital economy influenced our lives?
2. How do we take advantage of the digital economy?

Section B Public Speaking

Activity One

Read the passage below and get some knowledge about using visual aids.

Using Visual Aids

Using visual aids in public speaking is a way of enhancing your speech with objects, images, graphs, charts, slides, or other visual elements that can help your audience understand and remember your message better. Visual aids can also help you as a speaker by providing you with notes, structure, confidence, and credibility. Some benefits of using visual aids in public speaking are:

- Improving audience understanding and memory: Visual aids can make your speech

more clear, concrete, and memorable by showing rather than telling your points. Visual aids can also appeal to different learning styles and preferences of your audience members.
- Serving as notes: Visual aids can help you remember what to say next and keep you on track with your speech. Visual aids can also help you avoid reading from a script or relying on memorization.
- Providing clearer organization: Visual aids can help you structure your speech and show the relationships between your main points and subpoints. Visual aids can also help you signal transitions and emphasize key ideas.
- Facilitating more eye contact and motion by the speaker: Visual aids can encourage you to look at your audience more often and move around the stage or room more naturally. Visual aids can also help you engage your audience's attention and interest by creating variety and contrast in your speech.
- Contributing to speaker credibility: Visual aids can help you establish your authority and expertise on your topic by showing evidence, data, sources, or examples that support your claims. Visual aids can also help you appear more prepared, confident, and professional.

However, using visual aids in public speaking also requires careful planning, preparation, and practice. Some tips for using visual aids in public speaking are:
- Choosing visual aids that are relevant, visible, varied, attractive, and appropriate for your speech purpose, topic, audience, and occasion.
- Introducing your visual aids before showing them to your audience and explaining how they relate to your speech. Give your audience enough time to process the information in your visual aids but do not let them distract from your speech.
- Standing to the side of your visual aids and do not obscure them or turn your back to the audience. Maintain eye contact with your audience and use gestures or pointers to direct their attention to the key elements of your visual aids.
- Practicing with your visual aids and make sure they work properly and smoothly. Have a backup plan in case of technical difficulties or unexpected situations. Be flexible and adaptable to any changes or challenges that may arise during your speech.

Activity Two

Answer the following questions according to the passage above.
1. What is the function of using visual aids in public speaking?

2. What are the benefits of using visual aids in public speaking?

3. What are the tips for using visual aids in public speaking?

 **Activity Three**

Read a passage about some criteria to evaluate the quality of visual aids and complete the outline of it.

Criteria to Evaluate the Quality of Visual Aids

Visual aids can be an important part of conveying messages effectively since people learn far more by hearing and seeing than through hearing or seeing alone. However, visual aids should be used appropriately and effectively. Here are some criteria to evaluate the quality of visual aids:

Relevance

The visual aid should be directly related to the topic, purpose, and message of the presentation. It should not include any unnecessary or distracting information or images.

Clarity

The visual aid should be easy to read, understand, and follow. It should not have too much text, colors, or effects that may clutter or confuse the main message. It should also have appropriate labels, titles, captions, legends, or keys that explain what it shows and how it relates to the presentation.

Consistency

The visual aid should be consistent with the style, tone, and format of the presentation. It should also use consistent fonts, sizes, and styles that are visible and legible for the audience.

Attractiveness

The visual aid should be appealing and engaging for the audience. It should use colors, fonts, and shapes that are suitable for the topic and audience. It should also use visuals that are high-quality, original, or creative.

Integration

The visual aid should complement the speech, not replace it. It should be synchronized, relevant, and supportive of the main points and arguments of the presentation. It should also be used effectively with cues, transitions, and explanations.

Unit 10
Digital Economy

Criteria to Evaluate the Quality of Visual Aids	
Relevance	Related to the 1. _____, purpose, and message of the speech
Clarity	Easy to read, understand, and 2. _____
Consistency	Consistent with the 3. _____, tone, and format of the speech
Attractiveness	4. _____ and engaging for the audience
Integration	Complementing the speech, not 5. _____ it

Activity Four

Choose one of the following topics and deliver a public speech related to career development in the IT industry with the help of the public speaking skill above.
- ◆ IT career path
- ◆ IT skills and certifications
- ◆ IT networking and mentoring

Section C Further Listening

Activity One

Listen to a conversation between a student and an employee at the study-abroad office. Fill in each blank within three words.

1. What is the student's concern regarding his/her passport?
   Answer: The student is concerned about his/her passport _____ before he/she returns from studying abroad.

2. What suggestion does the employee give, regarding the passport issue?
   Answer: The employee advises the student to have his/her passport _____ before going abroad and suggests talking to the person in charge of the semester abroad program for further guidance.

3. Did the student miss the deadline for the spring semester abroad program in France?
   Answer: Yes, the student missed the deadline for the spring semester abroad program

in France, which was September _____.

4. Why does the student hesitate to study abroad next year?
   Answer: The student expresses hesitation about studying abroad next year because the student has plans to work on an independent study with his/her _____, Professor Jacobs, and cannot leave the country during that time.

5. What alternative option does the employee suggest for the student to study abroad in France?
   Answer: The employee suggests that the student can apply for the fall semester abroad program or consider studying abroad in France during the _____, which is a shorter duration.

6. What is the student's major?
   Answer: The student's major is French _____.

7. What is the deadline for the summer program in France?
   Answer: The employee mentions that the student should have _____ weeks until the deadline for the summer program, but it is emphasized that the program is popular and can fill up quickly.

8. Why does the employee express surprise that the student missed the spring semester deadline?
   Answer: The employee is surprised because it is _____ for language majors, like the student, to apply for study abroad programs to improve their language skills, and the student's advisor might have suggested it.

9. Who does the employee recommend the student to talk to about his/her study abroad plans?
   Answer: The employee recommends that the student speak to his/her advisor about his/her study abroad plans, as the advisor might have good advice and will need to write a(n) _____.

10. What final advice does the employee give to the student?
    Answer: The employee advises the student to talk to his/her _____, take the brochure for the program in France, and inform the study-abroad office if he/she has any more questions. The employee also emphasizes the importance of a good recommendation letter in the application process.

Unit 10
Digital Economy

Activity Two

You will hear a trainer talking to people who want to learn outdoor survival skills. Complete the outline by filling in each blank within three words.

Outdoor Survival Program

I. Introduction

Overview of the outdoor survival program.

Classroom-based learning followed by a(n) 1. _____.

II. Food Preparation Techniques

Introduction to two methods: steam pit and 2. _____.

Use of natural resources for cooking in the outdoors.

III. Steam Pit Cooking

Required materials: dry sticks, grass, loose earth, stones, and 3. _____ (for the week).

Steps:

- Digging a shallow pit of approximately 25cm deep and 30cm wide.
- Placing 4. _____ along the top of the pit.
- Arranging large stones on top of the sticks.
- Starting the fire and waiting for the 5. _____ to burn through.
- 6. _____ hot ash from the stones.
- Inserting a stick into the center of the pit between the stones.
- Covering the pit with a(n) 7. _____ of grass.
- 8. _____ food in grass and placing it on the grass layer.
- Covering the entire pit with earth and patting it firmly.
- Removing the stick and 9. _____ into the opening.
- Cooking time: approximately 10. _____ in the steam.

Activity Three

Listen to a passage about craftsmanship for making Chinese fans. Fill in each blank within three words.

Craftsmanship for Making Chinese Fans

Craftsmanship for making Chinese fans dates back to some three or four thousand years ago and features more than 400 varieties of hand fans. Chinese fans vary in their frames, coverings and shapes, even in the 1. _____ on them, treating the audience to a visual feast.

Chinese fans are mainly produced in four places, namely Jiangsu Province, Zhejiang Province, 2. _____ and Guangdong Province, three of which are situated along the Yangtze River.

The city of Hangzhou has been famous for its "elegant fans" since 3. _____. Its fan-making industry especially developed in the 4. _____ when the capital was moved to Lin'an (present-day Hangzhou). The Ming and Qing Dynasties witnessed a boom in the production of Hangzhou fans, which enjoy equal fame as silk and tea, boasted one of "the 5. _____ of Hangzhou".

Men of letters in all times love to write poems or 6. _____ on the covering of a fan. As a result, calligraphy and painting on fans have become a(n) 7. _____ over the last several hundred years. Since it requires outstanding craftsmanship and 8. _____, all artists take it as a challenge to their skills to draw on the covering of a fan. Since ancient times, great calligraphers and painters never 9. _____ in showing their talents by writing and painting on fans. Simple as it seems, the fan, with its strong cultural presence, is no longer just a daily utensil, but a work of art with both practical and 10. _____ values.

Unit 11
Technology and Work

Learning Objectives

In this unit, you will:
- learn about how technology transforms work;
- learn to grasp key information in a talk;
- learn to speak to persuade.

Background

In the digital age, technology has revolutionized the way we work, streamlined processes and automated tasks. The rise of artificial intelligence, machine learning, and robotics has led to increased efficiency, remote work opportunities, and new industries, while also raising concerns about job displacement and the future of human labor. As technology continues to advance, striking a balance between innovation and job security remains a key challenge.

Section A Listening

Pre-Listening

Work in pairs and discuss the following questions.

1. What do you think of flexible working?
2. To what extent do you think automation will outweigh humans?

Activity One

Work in small groups to discuss the following questions.

1. Where do you prefer to work, at the office or at home?
    A. At the office.
    B. At home.

2. Which way of communication do you like better?
    A. Face-to-face talk.
    B. Video calls.

3. Some argue that automation is not good for people's employment. Do you agree or not?
    A. Yes.
    B. No.

4. How does automation impact people's work?
    A. It affects people's occupations.

B. More people will have to work with technology.

C. Some workers may experience wage pressure.

D. All of the above.

5. Do you agree that technology brings more positive changes to the workplace than negative ones?

A. Yes.

B. No.

While-Listening

Text A Transforming the Workplace by Technology

Language Bank

hot-desking	['hɒt deskɪŋ]	n.	办公桌轮用制（按需要或依照轮流制度分配办公桌，而不是给每位员工桌子）
remote	[rɪ'məʊt]	adj.	远程的
optional	['ɒpʃənl]	adj.	可选择的
regardless	[rɪ'gɑːdləs]	adv.	不顾
streamline	['striːmlaɪn]	v.	精简（工商企业、组织、流程等）使效率更高
developer	[dɪ'veləpə(r)]	n.	开发者

Activity Two

You will hear a passage about how technology has transformed the workplace. Listen and choose the best answer to each question.

1. The following can all be used to describe flexible working EXCEPT _____.

   A. people needn't work at the office

   B. each employee has his own desk position

   C. employees can choose to work remotely

   D. flexibility is a fundamental requirement, not just an optional extra for sectors

2. What is TRUE about the video call?

   A. It is a new and better interaction way for teams.

   B. It promotes face-to-face meetings.

C. It has a time limit.

D. It can't cross geographical borders.

3. Which is NOT the advantage of automation?

   A. Some time-intensive business processes are being streamlined.

   B. Automation is time-consuming.

   C. Automation can make work efficient.

   D. People can focus on the really important work.

4. Which description of citizen developers is NOT true?

   A. They are a new type of employee.

   B. They create new business applications.

   C. They wait for IT to catch up with them.

   D. They have grown up in a technology-first world.

5. What is the passage mainly about?

   A. Technology changes people's lifestyles.

   B. Technology is everywhere.

   C. Technology changes people's workplaces.

   D. Technology provides jobs for developers.

Activity Three

Listen again and decide whether the following statements are true (T) or false (F).

( ) 1. It's time for businesses in all industries to embrace flexible working practices.

( ) 2. Teams that promote collaborative working are more likely to be high performing.

( ) 3. Automation helps businesses focus on mundane, time-intensive tasks.

( ) 4. Work-related apps can only be built by professional developers.

( ) 5. The Microsoft Power Platform is an example of a low code platform for citizen developers.

Unit 11
Technology and Work

Text B The Influence of Automation and Technology on Work

📞 Language Bank

occupation	[ˌɒkju'peɪʃən]	n.	职业
representative	[ˌreprɪ'zentətɪv]	n.	代表
labor	['leɪbə(r)]	n.	劳工
deployment	[dɪ'plɔɪmənt]	n.	部署
abundant	[ə'bʌndənt]	adj.	充足的
weigh	[weɪ]	v.	权衡
scenario	[sə'nɑːriəʊ]	n.	情景

Activity Four

You will hear a passage about the influence of automation and technology on work. Listen and choose the best answer to each question.

1. What percentage of occupations can be fully automated using the currently demonstrated technology?

   A. More than 50 percent.

   B. Approximately 30 percent.

   C. Less than 5 percent.

   D. Around 80 percent.

2. According to the research, which of the following occupations will be affected by automation?

   A. Factory workers and clerks only.

   B. Highly skilled workers exclusively.

   C. CEOs and fashion designers only.

   D. Various occupations including landscape gardeners and insurance sales representatives.

3. What percentage of all occupations have at least 30 percent of activities that are technically automatable?

   A. Around 10 percent.

   B. Approximately 40 percent.

C. Close to 60 percent.

D. More than 80 percent.

4. Which factor is mentioned as a consideration for the deployment of automation?

    A. Cost of hardware and software development.

    B. Supply-and-demand dynamics of labor.

    C. Technical feasibility of automation.

    D. All of the above.

5. According to the scenarios presented, how long might it take before automation reaches 50 percent of all of today's work activities?

    A. Less than a decade.

    B. At least two decades.

    C. More than three decades.

    D. It is not specified in the text.

Activity Five

Listen again and decide whether the following statements are true (T) or false (F).

(   ) 1. MGI research has examined more than 3,000 work activities and quantified the technical feasibility of automating each of them.

(   ) 2. Low-skilled workers working with technology will be able to achieve more in terms of output and productivity, and they will not experience wage pressure.

(   ) 3. The adoption of automation will pick up as machines become more advanced.

(   ) 4. Benefits of automation beyond labor substitution include higher levels of output, better quality and fewer errors, and capabilities that surpass human ability.

(   ) 5. Regulatory and social issues do not need to be weighed when it comes to automation.

Post-Listening

Work in pairs and discuss the following questions.

1. How is technology affecting the job market?

2. How can we work with automation?

Section B Public Speaking

 Activity One

Read the passage below and get some knowledge about speaking to persuade.

Speaking to Persuade

Speaking to persuade is a type of public speaking that aims to motivate the audience to take a specific action or adopt a certain viewpoint on a topic. It involves using solid arguments, moving language, and rhetorical strategies to appeal to the audience's logic, emotions, and values.

When speaking to persuade, the speaker typically employs various persuasive techniques such as:

- Establishing credibility: The speaker presents themselves as knowledgeable and trustworthy to gain the audience's confidence and respect.
- Using evidence: providing factual information, statistics, research findings, or expert opinions to support the speaker's claims and strengthen their argument.
- Appealing to emotions: utilizing emotional language, personal stories, vivid examples, or powerful visuals to evoke emotional responses and create a connection with the audience.
- Employing logical reasoning: presenting logical arguments, using deductive or inductive reasoning, and highlighting cause-and-effect relationships to demonstrate the validity of the speakers point of view.
- Addressing counterarguments: anticipating and addressing potential objections or opposing viewpoints to acknowledge the audience's concerns and strengthen the speaker's position.
- Utilizing persuasive language: employing rhetorical devices, such as repetition, parallelism, metaphors, or persuasive appeals (ethos, pathos, and logos), to make the speech more compelling and memorable.
- Structuring the speech effectively: organizing the speech in a coherent manner, with a clear introduction, well-developed body points, and a persuasive conclusion, to guide the audience through the argument and leave a lasting impression.

 **Activity Two**

Answer the following questions according to the passage above.

1. What is the aim of persuasive speaking?
2. What does persuasive speaking involve?
3. What persuasive techniques could be used in persuasive speaking?

 **Activity Three**

Read an example of a persuasive speech and complete the outline of it.

Education

Hello, everyone. My name is John, and I am here to talk to you about a topic that affects all of us: education. Education is not just about learning facts and skills in school. It is also about developing our minds, our personalities, and our values. It is about becoming better citizens, better workers, and better human beings. Education is the key to our personal and collective success.

Why do I say that? Because education has many benefits for individuals and society. Let me share some of them with you.

First, education improves our personal well-being and development. Studies have shown that people with higher levels of education tend to have higher incomes, better health, longer life expectancy, and more happiness than those with lower levels of education. Education also helps us develop our critical thinking, creativity, and problem-solving skills, which are essential for facing the challenges and opportunities of the 21st century.

Second, education promotes social justice and equality. Education can help reduce poverty, discrimination, and violence by empowering people with knowledge, skills, and opportunities. Education can also foster tolerance, respect, and dialogue among people from different backgrounds, cultures, and beliefs. Education can help us overcome ignorance, prejudice, and hatred that divide us.

Third, education contributes to economic growth and development. Education can boost productivity, innovation, and competitiveness by providing people with the human capital they need to succeed in the global market. Education can also create more jobs, reduce unemployment, and increase tax revenues by expanding the labor force and the consumer base. Education can help us achieve a more prosperous and sustainable future.

As you can see, education is vital for our individual and collective well-being. But unfortunately, not everyone has access to quality education. According to UNESCO, there are still 258 million children and youth out of school worldwide. There are also millions of adults who lack basic literacy and numeracy skills. And there are many barriers that prevent people from pursuing higher education, such as cost, distance, or discrimination.

This is unacceptable. We cannot afford to waste the potential of millions of people who could contribute to our society if they had access to education. We cannot allow the gap between the educated and the uneducated to widen and create more inequality and injustice. We cannot ignore the moral and human right of every person to receive an education.

That is why I urge you to join me in supporting education for all. Education for All is a global movement that aims to ensure that every child, youth, and adult has access to quality education regardless of their circumstances. Education for All is also a personal commitment that each one of us can make to value education in our own lives and in the lives of others.

How can we do that? Here are some ways.

We can support organizations that provide educational opportunities for disadvantaged groups, such as girls, refugees, or people with disabilities. We can volunteer as tutors, mentors, or teachers for students who need extra help or guidance. We can donate books, supplies, or funds to schools or libraries that lack resources. We can advocate for policies and reforms that improve the quality and accessibility of education at local, national, or international levels. We can encourage our friends, family members, or colleagues to pursue their educational goals or aspirations. We can continue learning throughout our lives by taking courses, reading books, or exploring new interests.

These are just some examples of how we can support education for all. There are many more ways we can get involved and make a difference. The important thing is that we act now and not later. Because every day counts. Every day is an opportunity to learn something new or teach something valuable. Every day is an opportunity to change someone's life or change the world.

Remember: Education is not a privilege; it is a right. Education is not a luxury; it is a necessity. Education is not a burden; it is a blessing.

Thank you for your attention!

Education	
Introduction	A. Greeting and introducing oneself (John) B. Stating the topic: education and its significance for individuals and society

(Continued)

	Education
Importance of education	A. Personal well-being and 1. _____ • Higher incomes, better health, longer life expectancy, and happiness • Development of critical thinking, creativity, and problem-solving skills B. Social justice and equality • Poverty reduction, 2. _____, and opportunity creation • Fostering tolerance, respect, and dialogue among diverse groups C. Economic growth and development • Boosting productivity, innovation, and competitiveness • Creating jobs, 3. _____ unemployment, and increasing tax revenues
Education disparities and challenges	A. Number of children and youth out of school (258 million) B. Adults lacking basic literacy and numeracy skills C. Barriers to pursuing 4. _____ education (cost, distance, discrimination)
Call to action: education for all	A. Supporting the global movement for education for all B. Personal commitments to value education • Supporting disadvantaged groups and organizations • Volunteering as tutors, mentors, or teachers • Donating resources to schools or libraries • Advocating for educational policies and reforms • Encouraging others to pursue educational goals • Lifelong 5. _____ opportunities for personal growth
Conclusion	A. Reinforcing the importance of education as a right and necessity B. Thanking the audience for their attention

Activity Four

Choose one of the topics below and deliver a persuasive speech related to technology with the help of the public speaking skill above.

◆ The benefits of AI in healthcare
◆ The importance of data privacy
◆ The dangers of technological addiction

Unit 11
Technology and Work

Section C Further Listening

Activity One

Listen to a conversation between a student and his chemistry professor. Fill in each blank within three words.

1. What was the student's original research project idea?
   Answer: The student's original research project idea was to work on _____ derived from organic materials, biofuel.

2. Why did the student decide to work on a project involving glycerol?
   Answer: The student found out that in the process of making biofuel, there is a lot of leftover material after processing the corn or sugar or whatever into fuel. And most of those byproducts are just _____, all the way to landfills.

3. What are some industrial uses for glycerol mentioned in the conversation?
   Answer: Glycerol is a common ingredient in _____ and some food products.

4. What was the idea the student read about involving glycerol and grass seed?
   Answer: The idea was to make a really _____ that can be put on grass seed, so they stick to the ground and that would give them more time to germinate.

5. What does the student ask the professor for help with?
   Answer: The student asks the professor if they can use one of the _____ in Hazelton Hall to grow grass.

6. Why does the student need a lot of space to grow grass?
   Answer: The student needs a lot of space to grow grass because Hazelton's is the only place that is set up to grow lots of plants under _____, indoors.

7. What does the professor suggest the student work on, instead of field testing the sticky film?
   Answer: The professor suggests that the student work on _____ the sticky film instead.

8. Why does the student want to field test the sticky film on grass seed?
   Answer: The student wants to know if the sticky film _____.

9. What does the student hope to achieve by finding a new use for glycerol?
   Answer: The student hopes to find a(n) _____ for glycerol so that the waste

byproducts produced from making biofuel can be minimized.

10. Does the professor agree to sponsor the student's research?

    Answer: The conversation does not provide a clear answer as to whether the professor agrees to sponsor the student's research. However, the professor offers to see if they can get the student access to Hazelton, although they caution the student not to get their _____ up.

Activity Two

You will hear a university lecturer talking about fast food consumption to a class of students. Complete the outline by filling in each blank within three words.

The Problems Associated with Fast Food Consumption

I. Introduction

Fast food consumption has increased among middle-class people in most countries from 2001 to 2005.

II. Fast food consumption trends in different countries

- Japan: traditionally resisted fast food, but by 2005, Japanese people were eating 1. _____ fast food meals per week.
- Korea: fast food consumption remained the same from 2. _____, but increased to four meals per week in 2005.
- 3. _____ : similar results in 2001 and 2003, but a smaller increase in 2005 than Korea.
- England: Fast food used to be 4. _____ among lower socioeconomic groups, but middle-class consumption increased from 2001 to 2003 and continued to increase in 2005.
- Australia: Middle-class consumption increased from three meals per week in 2001 to 5. _____ meals per week in 2005.

III. Health implications of fast food consumption

High levels of fast food consumption are 6. _____ to people's health.

- Young people under 7. _____ are worst affected with diabetes and respiratory illnesses, and difficulty with concentration and 8. _____ memory loss.
- People in their mid-20s up to their 9. _____ have a high incidence of diabetes and

cardiac problems.
- People in their mid-fifties and over experience cardiac illness, and evidence shows that fast food worsens 10. _____ around this time of life.

Activity Three

Listen to a passage about Chinese culture and complete the outline by filling in each blank within three words.

What Makes the Chinese Culture?

I. Introduction

A. Chinese culture as the joint creation of all ethnic groups

B. Inclusiveness as the key characteristic of Chinese culture

II. **Cultural Contributions of Ethnic Groups**

A. Literary works
- *The Book of Songs*
- The 1. _____
- Poetry in the Han Dynasty
- Poetry of the Tang Dynasty
- Song Poems
- Opera from the Yuan Dynasty
- Novels of the 2. _____ and Qing Dynasties

B. Epic works
- *The Epic of King Gesar*
- *The Epic of Manas*
- *The Epic of Jangar*

C. Architectural achievements
- 3. _____
- Dujiangyan ancient irrigation system
- 4. _____
- Imperial Palace
- Potala Palace
- Qanat water 5. _____ system

III. **Chinese Socialism in a New Era**

A. Optimistic outlook for development

B. Challenges in domestic and 6. _____ situations

C. The need for unity and strength

IV. Ethnic Unity as a Fundamental Task

A. All ethnic groups as one 7. _____

B. Enhancing the sense of Chinese 8. _____

C. Implementation of the Party's theories and policies

D. Working together for 9. _____ and development

V. Conclusion

A. A more 10. _____ and cohesive Chinese nation

B. Fulfilling the Chinese Dream through ethnic unity and progress

Unit 12

Big Data

Learning Objectives

In this unit, you will:
- learn about the application of big data;
- learn to listen for detailed information in a talk;
- learn to speak to inform.

Background

As the digital landscape expands with the rise of social media and other communication channels, companies are faced with an abundance of data from customer feedback and behavior. To stay competitive, organizations are turning to big data analytics to gain insights into customer sentiment and behavior, which can help improve operations, enhance customer experience, and drive business value. By leveraging the power of big data, companies can analyze customer feedback and behavior to deliver personalized recommendations, targeted marketing campaigns, and more.

Section A Listening

Pre-Listening

Work in pairs and discuss the following questions.
1. Where does big data come from?
2. What are some common challenges associated with big data?

Activity One

There are several statements about big data. Decide whether they are true (T) or false (F).

(　　) 1. The importance of big data simply revolves around how much data you have.

(　　) 2. The value of big data lies in how you use it.

(　　) 3. By taking data from any source and analyzing it, you can find answers that enable smart decision-making.

(　　) 4. While traditional data is measured in familiar sizes like petabytes and zettabytes, big data is stored in megabytes, gigabytes, and terabytes.

(　　) 5. Everything from emails and videos to scientific and meteorological data can constitute a big data stream, each with its own unique attributes.

(　　) 6. Our phones, credit cards, software applications, vehicles, records, websites and the majority of "things" in our world are capable of transmitting vast amounts of data, but this information is not very valuable.

(　　) 7. Companies and organizations must have the capabilities to harness this data and generate insights from it in real-time, otherwise it's not very useful.

(　　) 8. Big data analytics is used in nearly every industry to identify patterns and trends, answer questions, gain insights into customers and tackle complex problems.

While-Listening

Text A　The Advantages of Big Data

Language Bank

carjacker	['kɑːdʒækə(r)]	n.	劫车者
feathery	['feðəri]	adj.	柔软如羽毛的
quill	[kwɪl]	n.	大翎毛
inkwell	['ɪŋkwel]	n.	墨水池
telecommunication	[ˌtelɪkəˌmjuːnɪ'keɪʃn]	n.	电讯
telltale	['telteɪl]	n.	迹象
biopsy	['baɪɒpsi]	n.	活组织检查
cancerous	['kænsərəs]	adj.	癌的
biochemistry	[baɪəʊ'kemɪstri]	n.	生物化学
automation	[ˌɔːtə'meɪʃn]	n.	自动化
microscope	['maɪkrəskəʊp]	n.	显微镜
stakeholder	['steɪkhəʊldə(r)]	n.	利益相关者
render into			译成 (某种语言)

Activity Two

You will hear a long passage about big data. Decide whether the following statements are true (T) or false (F).

(　　) 1. In modern society, we still need the discs to store the information.

(　　) 2. Files that Edward Snowden took from the National Security Agency are heavy.

(　　) 3. The disc that's 4,000 years old doesn't store a lot of information, but the information is unchangeable.

(　　) 4. Your location information only could be recorded with a cell phone that has a GPS.

(　　) 5. With the help of big data, a non-approved driver could start the car.

Activity Three

Listen to the complete passage and choose the best answer to each question.

1. What is the difference between the information stored in these two kind of "discs"?

    A. We can store the same information as before.

    B. The information is heavier.

    C. The information could be used more easily.

    D. The information could be saved for longer than before.

2. According to the passage, which one of the following statements is the value of big data?

    A. People can do things that they want.

    B. To help the computer to figure out problems for itself.

    C. To follow Martin Luther at all times.

    D. To type a password into the dashboard.

3. According to the passage, which kind of functions could be achieved on the basis of machine learning?

    A. Collecting information.

    B. Voice recognition.

    C. Recording your location.

    D. Video chat.

4. According to the passage, which one is NOT the dark side of big data?

    A. The police could send the patrols according to the records.

    B. We may be punished for invasion of privacy.

    C. Big data is going to steal our jobs.

    D. Big data is going to challenge the white collar.

5. What is the challenge in the big data age?

    A. To protect our privacy.

    B. To protect our jobs.

    C. To safeguard free will, moral choice, and other human rights.

    D. To safeguard the security of the world.

Unit 12 Big Data

Text B The Application of Big Data

Language Bank

sentiment	['sentɪmənt]	n.	情感
feedback	['fi:dbæk]	v.	反馈
Hadoop	[hædu:p]	n.	分布式计算
outperform	[ˌaʊtpə'fɔ:m]	v.	超过
leverage	['li:vərɪdʒ]	v.	发挥
forum	['fɔ:rəm]	n.	论坛
harness	['hɑ:nɪs]	v.	控制
tenfold	['tenfəʊld]	adj.	十倍的

Activity Four

You will hear a passage about the application of big data. Listen and decide whether the following statements are true (T) or false (F).

(　　) 1. IT is important for organizations to know and analyze customers' evaluations of their products or services.

(　　) 2. Big data analytics helps organizations respond quickly to emerging problems.

(　　) 3. Airlines use behavioral analytics to improve customer experience.

(　　) 4. Organizations use behavioral analytics to add value to their business through predicting customer behavior.

(　　) 5. McDonald's is using big data analytics to optimize its operations and enhance customer experience.

Activity Five

Listen to the passage again and fill in each blank within three words.

When it comes to customer sentiment analysis, big data can be used to analyze customer feedback, 1. _____ and comments across various communication channels. By leveraging commercial Hadoop distributions, companies can 2. _____ on social media and forums, enabling them to respond quickly to emerging problems and build positive brand recognition. The outcome of sentiment analysis is less 3. _____ and is beneficial to advertising programs, marketing programs and 4. _____. For example, airlines use sentiment analysis to analyze 5. _____ and respond accordingly, such as offering upgrades or resolving issues related to lost baggage.

Behavioral analytics, on the other hand, helps companies understand customer 6. _____ and preferences. By analyzing customer data, companies can predict customer behavior and offer personalized recommendations. For example, Amazon uses behavioral analytics to 7. _____ products based on customer interests, while other companies like Spotify, Pinterest, and Netflix follow suit. McDonald's also uses 8. _____ to optimize its restaurant operations, analyzing data on factors such as 9. _____, information on the menu, the size of the orders and 10. _____ to enhance customer experience.

Post-Listening

Work in pairs and discuss the following questions.

1. How can students prepare themselves for a career in the field of big data?
2. What are some ethical considerations that companies must take into account when collecting and analyzing big data?

Section B Public Speaking

Activity One

Read the passage below and get some knowledge about speaking to inform.

Speaking to Inform

Speaking to inform is a type of public speaking that aims to teach or instruct the audience about a topic. It uses descriptions, demonstrations, and strong details to explain a person, place, or subject. An informative speech makes a complex topic easier to understand and focuses on delivering information, rather than providing a persuasive argument.

Some general categories of informative speaking topics are objects, processes, events and concepts. Informative speeches on objects focus on things existing in the world, such as people, places, animals, or products. Informative speeches on processes focus on patterns of action, such as how something works or how to do something. Informative speeches on events focus on occurrences that happened in the past, are happening in the present, or will happen in the future. Informative speeches on concepts focus on abstract ideas or theories that may not have a concrete existence.

A good informative speech should contain the following elements:
- A clear and specific purpose statement that tells the audience what they will learn from the speech.
- A well-researched and organized content that covers the main points of the topic and provides relevant and reliable information.
- A catchy introduction that grabs the audience's attention, establishes the credibility, and previews the main points.
- A smooth transition between each main point that helps the audience follow the speech and understand how the points are connected.
- A memorable conclusion that summarizes your main points, reinforces your purpose, and leaves a lasting impression on the audience.
- A clear and confident delivery that uses appropriate vocal and nonverbal cues, such as eye contact, gestures, tone, and pace.
- A visual aid or example that enhances your speech and helps the audience visualize or understand your information better.

Activity Two

Answer the following questions according to the passage above.
1. What is the aim of informative speaking?
2. What are the general categories of informative speaking?
3. What should a good informative speech contain?

Activity Three

Read one example of an informative speech and complete the outline of it.

The Benefits of Meditation

Good afternoon, everyone.

Have you ever felt stressed, anxious, or overwhelmed by the challenges of life? If so, you are not alone. According to the American Psychological Association, 77% of Americans experience stress that affects their physical health, and 73% experience stress that affects their mental health. Stress can have negative impacts on your mood, memory, sleep, immune system, and cardiovascular health. Therefore, finding ways to cope with stress is essential for your well-being.

I have been practicing meditation for over five years and I have learned a lot from books, podcasts, and online courses. I have also experienced the benefits of meditation firsthand in terms of reducing stress, enhancing focus, and boosting happiness. In this speech, I will explain what meditation is, how it works, and why it is good for your health and well-being.

Let's start by defining what meditation is. Meditation is a practice of focusing your attention on a single object, such as your breath, a word, or a sound. Meditation requires concentration and awareness. Concentration means keeping your attention on one thing at a time and bringing it back when it wanders. Awareness means being aware of your thoughts, feelings, sensations, and surroundings without reacting to them.

Now that we know what meditation is, let's see how it works. Meditation works by changing the activity and structure of your brain. Meditation affects the activity of your brain waves and neurotransmitters. Meditation can increase the activity of alpha and theta brain waves that are associated with relaxation and creativity. Meditation can also increase the levels of neurotransmitters such as serotonin and dopamine that are associated with happiness and motivation.

Meditation affects the structure of your brain regions and connections. Meditation can increase the size and density of brain regions such as the hippocampus and the prefrontal cortex that are involved in learning and executive functions. Meditation can also increase the strength and efficiency of brain connections such as the corpus callosum and the default mode network that are involved in coordination and self-awareness.

Now that we know how meditation works, let's see why it is good for your health and well-being. Meditation can improve your mental and physical health in various ways. Meditation can reduce stress and anxiety by lowering your cortisol levels and activating your parasympathetic nervous system. Meditation can improve your mood and cognition by increasing your serotonin and dopamine levels and strengthening your brain regions and connections. Meditation can boost your immune system and cardiovascular health by decreasing inflammation and improving blood flow and oxygen delivery.

Meditation can improve your mental and physical health in various ways. As the famous meditation teacher Jon Kabat-Zinn said, "You can't stop the waves, but you can learn to surf."

Meditation can help you surf the waves of life with more ease, joy, and resilience.

The Benefits of Meditation	
Introduction	A. Acknowledging the prevalence of stress and its impact on health B. Stating the purpose of the speech: exploring the benefits of meditation for stress reduction and well-being
Definition of meditation	A. Describing meditation as a practice of focused attention on a(n) 1. _____ object B. Explaining the importance of concentration and awareness in meditation
How meditation works	A. Changing brain 2. _____ through brain waves and neurotransmitters B. Modifying brain structure and connections
Benefits of meditation for health and well-being	A. Reducing 3. _____ and anxiety B. Improving mood and cognition C. Boosting 4. _____ system and cardiovascular health
Conclusion	A. Summarizing the key points of the speech B. Emphasizing the role of meditation in navigating life's challenges with ease, joy, and 5. _____

Activity Four

Choose one of the following topics and deliver an informative speech related to the IT industry with the help of the public speaking skill above.

◆ The history and evolution of the IT industry
◆ The current trends and issues in the IT industry
◆ The future prospects and implications of the IT industry

Section C Further Listening

Activity One

Listen to a conversation between a student and an employee in the student affairs office. Fill in each blank within three words.

1. What is the student's new role?
   Answer: The student has been elected as the _____ of the Student Activities Board.

2. What is the student's idea for an event?
   Answer: The student wants to book the _____ for a campus-wide event.

3. What is the employee's initial response to the idea?
   Answer: The employee says that the student will need to _____ the band to come to their campus.

4. Why does the student think they can book the band?
   Answer: The band is performing in a(n) _____, and one of the members is an alumnus of the student's university.

5. What does Susan compare the sound of the Jimmy Smith Band to?
   Answer: The _____.

6. What is the first step the student needs to take to get funding for the event?
   Answer: The student needs to come up with _____ and fill out an application form to request funding.

7. What is the reason for the lack of funds on campus?
   Answer: The costs for last year's community outreach day were much _____ than expected.

8. Why does the employee suggest against a car wash fundraiser?
   Answer: The amount of money the student group would make would be _____ compared with the cost of cleaning supplies.

9. What fundraising idea does the employee suggest instead?
   Answer: The employee suggests an auction where local businesses _____ to sell for the highest bidder.

10. What does the student ask for at the end of the conversation?

    Answer: The student asks for the _____ who told the employee about the successful auction fundraiser at another university.

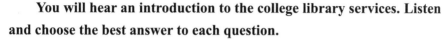 Activity Two

You will hear an introduction to the college library services. Listen and choose the best answer to each question.

1. Where can you find audio and video material?
   A. In the library.
   B. In the self-access language center.
   C. Both A and B.
   D. None of the above.

2. How many study places are available in the library?
   A. Approximately 100.
   B. Approximately 200.
   C. Approximately 300.
   D. Approximately 400.

3. Where are the general loan books located?
   A. Ground floor.
   B. First floor.
   C. Second floor.
   D. Basement.

4. Can reference books be taken out of the library?
   A. Yes, under certain conditions.
   B. No, under any circumstances.
   C. Yes, for full-time students only.
   D. Yes, for a maximum of three weeks.

5. What equipment is available in the library?
   A. Photocopy machines and microfilm readers.
   B. Engineering drawing boards and typewriters.
   C. Light table and tape-slide units.
   D. All of the above.

Activity Three

Listen to a passage about traditional firing technology. Complete the outline by filling in each blank within three words.

The Traditional Firing Technology of Longquan Celadon

Longquan is a historic and cultural city in Zhejiang Province, well-known for its celadon industry. There were 1. _____ famous kilns in the Chinese history, namely Guan, Ge, Ru, Ding, and Jun, among which Ge referred to the celadon kiln in Longquan.

Longquan kiln has the 2. _____ history, the widest distribution, the best quality and the broadest 3. _____ and export scope among all the celadon kilns in the Chinese ceramic history. Longquan celadon industry, dating back to the Western 4. _____ began to take shape in the Northern Song Dynasty, reached its prime in the 5. _____ and later periods of the Southern Song Dynasty, saw a(n) 6. _____ in quality during the Ming Dynasty with a production scale as large as before, and finally met its 7. _____ in the Qing Dynasty. Since the founding of the People's Republic of China, the firing technology of Longquan celadon has gradually 8. _____.

Celadon firing is a technology as well as an art. Celadon of the best quality, with its soft luster, rich flavor and 9. _____ beauty, carries a profound cultural connotation.

In 10. _____, the traditional firing technology of Longquan celadon was inscribed on the Representative List of the Intangible Cultural Heritage of Humanity by the UNESCO.

Unit 13

Algorithmic Bias

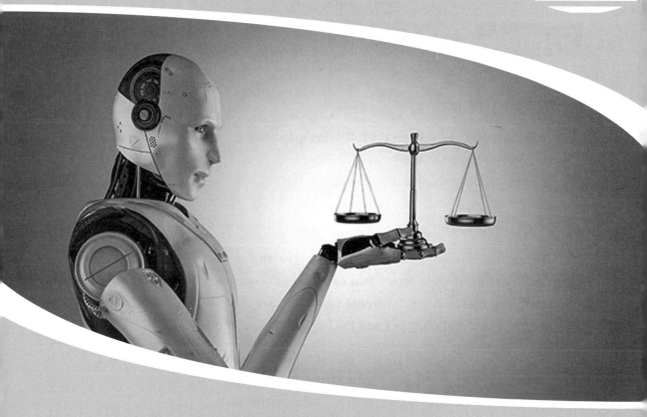

Learning Objectives

In this unit, you will:

- learn about algorithmic bias;
- learn to listen for specific information in a talk;
- learn to speak to motivate.

Background

Are algorithms and artificial intelligence inherently prejudiced? Do Facebook, Google, and Twitter have political biases? Those answers are complicated. But if the question is whether the tech industry is doing enough to address these biases, the straightforward response is no.

Section A Listening

Pre-Listening

Work in pairs and discuss the following questions.
1. What is algorithmic bias?
2. What would be the impact of algorithmic bias?

Activity One

There is a common concern about algorithmic bias which is described as systematic and repeatable errors that create unfair outcomes. Then what are the types of algorithmic bias? Also, what would be the impact of algorithmic bias? Put a "√" in the bracket in front of the types and the impact of algorithmic bias.

Types of algorithmic bias	(　) 1. Pre-existing bias (　) 2. Technical bias (　) 3. Emergent bias (　) 4. Correlations (　) 5. Unanticipated uses
Impact of algorithmic bias	(　) 6. Commercial influences (　) 7. Voting behavior (　) 8. Gender discrimination (　) 9. Racial and ethnic discrimination (　) 10. Disability discrimination

While-Listening

Text A An Introduction to Algorithmic Bias

Language Bank

algorithmic	[ˌælgə'rɪðəmɪk]	adj.	算法的
bias	['baɪəs]	n.	偏好
neutral	['njuːtrəl]	adj.	中立的
perpetuate	[pə'petʃueɪt]	v.	使持续
oppression	[ə'preʃn]	n.	压迫
aggravate	['ægrəveɪt]	v.	使更严重
supremacy	[suː'preməsi]	n.	最好
penalize	['piːnəlaɪz]	v.	使处于不利地位
demote	[diː'məʊt]	v.	使降级

Activity Two

You will hear an introduction to algorithmic bias. Listen and choose the best answer to each question.

1. What is the passage mainly about?

   A. Artificial intelligence.

   B. Algorithms.

   C. Algorithmic bias.

   D. Robots.

2. The following can all be used to describe algorithmic bias EXCEPT _____.

   A. it is also known as machine learning bias

   B. it refers to the tendency of algorithms to reflect human biases

   C. it arises when an algorithm delivers systematically biased results as a consequence of erroneous assumptions of the machine learning process

   D. it will not become more problematic

3. Why did the AI systems trained on non-representative data in healthcare typically perform poorly for underrepresented populations?

   A. Because an algorithm used in US hospitals to predict which patients will require additional medical care favored white patients over black patients by a considerable margin.

B. Because the algorithm considered the patients' past healthcare expenditures.

C. Because black individuals with similar diseases spent more on healthcare than white patients with similar issues.

D. Because the algorithm favored the white individuals and will continue to discriminate against black individuals.

4. How can we tell Amazon's hiring algorithm is biased towards women?

   A. Amazon's algorithm demoted applications of those who attended one of two all-female institutions.

   B. Amazon's computer models can spot similarities in candidates' applications.

   C. Amazon's recruiting tool utilized AI to assign job applicants ratings ranging from one to five stars.

   D. Amazon's algorithm evaluated applicants for software development jobs and other technical positions in a gender-neutral manner.

5. All of the following have been mentioned EXCEPT _____.

   A. the definition of algorithmic bias

   B. the examples of algorithmic bias

   C. the impact of algorithmic bias

   D. the solutions to deal with algorithmic bias

Activity Three

Listen again and decide whether the following statements are true (T) or false (F).

(   ) 1. Algorithmic bias is not machine learning bias.

(   ) 2. A facial recognition algorithm could be trained to recognize a white person more easily than a black person because this type of data has been used in training less often.

(   ) 3. In 2016, researchers found that an algorithm used in US hospitals to predict which patients would require additional medical care favored white patients over black patients by a considerable margin.

(   ) 4. Automation has played a critical role in Amazon's e-commerce supremacy.

(   ) 5. Recruiters used the tool's suggestions to find new employees and depended entirely on those rankings.

Text B Ways of Avoiding Algorithm Bias

Language Bank

counterfactual	[ˌkaʊntə'fæktʃuəl]	adj.	与事实相反的
orientation	[ˌɔːriən'teɪʃn]	n.	特别喜好
subsequent	['sʌbsɪkwənt]	adj.	随后的
multidisciplinary	[ˌmʌltidɪsə'plɪnəri]	adj.	跨学科的
address	[ə'dres]	v.	处理
verify	['verɪfaɪ]	v.	证实

Activity Four

You will hear a passage about how to avoid algorithmic bias. Listen and decide whether the following statements are true (T) or false (F).

(　　) 1. Your AI-powered solution might not be trustworthy if you apply AI to similar applicants.

(　　) 2. "Counterfactual fairness" can help guarantee a model's choices are the same in a counterfactual world where general characteristics like race, gender, or sexual orientation have been altered.

(　　) 3. When a machine cannot solve an issue, humans must interfere and solve the problem for them.

(　　) 4. Craig S. Smith argues that we need to reform science and technology education.

(　　) 5. Some problems may require not only technological answers, but also a multi-disciplinary approach, with views from ethicists, social scientists, and other humanities scholars.

Activity Five

Listen to the passage again and fill in each blank within three words.

How to Avoid Algorithm Bias

I. Testing Algorithms in a Real-Life Setting

◆ AI-powered solution might not be 1. _____ when the data comes from a specific group of job seekers.

- To deal with the issues, the algorithm should be tested in a manner 2. _____ to how it would be utilized in the real world.

II. Accounting for So-Called Counterfactual Fairness
- The definition of "fairness" and how it is computed are both up for discussion.
- Researchers work on methods that could 3. _____ that AI systems can satisfy "fairness".
- Pre-processing data
- Modifying the system's choices after the fact
- 4. _____ fairness definitions into the training process
- "Counterfactual fairness" is a potential approach to that.

III. Considering Human-in-the-Loop Systems
- The goal is to do what neither a human being nor a computer can 5. _____ on their own.
- When a machine cannot solve an issue, humans must interfere. Consequently, a continuous feedback loop will be created, and the system learns and improves its performance with each subsequent run, leading to more accurate rare datasets and improved safety and 6. _____.

IV. Changing the Way People Are Educated About Science and Technology
- Craig S. Smith believes it also takes a(n) 7. _____ change in the way people are educated about technology and science.
- There needs to be more multidisciplinary collaboration and rethinking of education.
- Some issues should be addressed and agreed upon 8. _____.
- Other issues should be addressed locally.

V. Summary
- Changes such as these would be 9. _____, but some problems may require more than technological answers and need a multidisciplinary approach.
- These changes alone may not help out in situations, if completely 10. _____ decision-making should be permitted at all in certain circumstances.

Post-Listening

Work in pairs and discuss the following questions.

1. What do you think of algorithmic bias?
2. How can you deal with algorithmic bias?

Section B Public Speaking

 **Activity One**

Read the passage below and get some knowledge about speaking to motivate.

Speaking to Motivate

Speaking to motivate is a type of public speaking that aims to inspire and persuade the audience to take action or change their behavior or attitude. It is a powerful way to communicate a message that resonates with people and can have a positive impact on their lives or environment. Some examples of speaking to motivate are graduation speeches, keynote speeches, TED talks, and motivational videos.

The following are some traits of a good motivational speech:

- A clear purpose: A good motivational speech has a clear and specific goal that it wants to achieve. It focuses on one main message that is relevant and meaningful to the audience.
- A personal story: A good motivational speech uses anecdotes and examples from the speaker's own life or from other people's lives to illustrate and support the main message. A personal story can make the speech more authentic, relatable, and memorable.
- A call to action: A good motivational speech ends with a strong and clear call to action that urges the audience to take a specific step or change their behavior, attitude, or beliefs in line with the main message.
- Passion and enthusiasm: A good motivational speaker must be passionate and enthusiastic about what they do and what they say. They must convey their emotions and energy to the audience and make them feel excited and inspired.
- Confidence and credibility: A good motivational speaker must be confident and credible in their delivery and content. They must speak with authority, conviction, and confidence, and back up their claims with data, facts, or testimonials.
- Empathy and selflessness: A good motivational speaker must be empathetic and selfless towards the audience. They must understand their needs, interests, and challenges, and tailor their speech to address them. They must also show that they care about the audience's well-being and success, and not just their own.
- Humor and engagement: A good motivational speaker must be humorous and engaging with the audience. They must use humor, stories, and effective language to capture the

audience's attention, break the ice, and make them laugh. They must also interact with the audience, ask questions, solicit feedback, and adapt to their reactions.

Activity Two

Answer the following questions according to the passage above.
1. What is the aim of motivational speaking?
2. Why is motivational speaking powerful?
3. What are some traits of a good motivational speech?

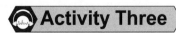
Activity Three

Read one example of a motivational speech and complete the outline of it.

Try Something New for 30 Days

A few years ago, I felt like I was stuck in a rut, so I decided to follow in the footsteps of the great American philosopher, Morgan Spurlock, and try something new for 30 days. The idea is actually pretty simple. Think about something you've always wanted to add to your life and try it for the next 30 days. It turns out 30 days is just about the right amount of time to add a new habit or subtract a habit—like watching the news—from your life.

There's a few things I learned while doing these 30-day challenges. The first was, instead of the months flying by, forgotten, the time was much more memorable. This was part of a challenge I did to take a picture every day for a month. And I remember exactly where I was and what I was doing that day. I also noticed that as I started to do more and harder 30-day challenges, my self-confidence grew. I went from desk-dwelling computer nerd to the kind of guy who bikes to work. For fun! Even last year, I ended up hiking up Mt. Kilimanjaro, the highest mountain in Africa. I would never have been that adventurous before I started my 30-day challenges.

I also figured out that if you really want something badly enough, you can do anything for 30 days. Have you ever wanted to write a novel? Every November, tens of thousands of people try to write their own 50,000-word novel, from scratch, in 30 days. It turns out, all you have to do is write 1,667 words a day for a month. So I did. By the way, the secret is not to go to sleep until you've written your words for the day. You might be sleep-deprived, but you'll finish your novel. Now is my book the next great American novel? No. I wrote it in a month. It's awful.

Unit 13
Algorithmic Bias

But for the rest of my life, if I meet John Hodgman at a TED party, I don't have to say, "I'm a computer scientist." No, no, if I want to, I can say, "I'm a novelist."

So here's one last thing I'd like to mention. I learned that when I made small, sustainable changes, things I could keep doing, they were more likely to stick. There's nothing wrong with big, crazy challenges. In fact, they're a ton of fun. But they're less likely to stick. When I gave up sugar for 30 days, day 31 looked like this.

So here's my question to you: What are you waiting for? I guarantee you the next 30 days are going to pass whether you like it or not, so why not think about something you have always wanted to try and give it a shot! For the next 30 days.

Thanks.

	Try Something New for 30 Days
Introduction	A. Personal experience: feeling in a rut and seeking change B. Inspired by Morgan Spurlock's concept of trying something new for 30 days
Memorable time and self-confidence	A. Taking a(n) 1. _____ every day for a month B. Increasing 2. _____ through challenging 30-day goals C. Transition from a desk-dweller to an adventurous individual
The power of 30 days	A. Achieving anything in 30 days B. Example of writing a(n) 3. _____ in a month
Small sustainable changes	A. The value of small, manageable changes B. Long-term 4. _____ and sustainability
Conclusion and call to action	A. Embracing the next 30 days as an opportunity for change B. Encouragement to pursue a desired 5. _____ or activity

Activity Four

Choose one of the following topics and deliver a motivational speech about cultivating a new hobby with the help of the public speaking skill above.

◆ Learning a new language
◆ Playing an instrument
◆ Learning photography

Section C Further Listening

Activity One

You will hear a talk about health. Listen and choose the best answer to each question.

1. Which food group contains large amounts of vitamins, minerals, fiber, and water?

    A. Fruits and vegetables.

    B. Whole grains.

    C. Meat and dairy products.

    D. Sugary snacks.

2. How can one increase fiber intake in their diet?

    A. Reduce fruit and vegetable consumption.

    B. Avoid whole grains.

    C. Eat more raw or lightly cooked vegetables.

    D. Consume more refined grains and processed foods.

3. Which fruits contain compounds that appear to protect against cancer?

    A. Apples and bananas.

    B. Berries and grapes.

    C. Citrus fruits.

    D. Deep oranges and strawberries.

4. How many servings of vegetables per day are recommended?

    A. 2 servings.

    B. 3 servings.

    C. 5 servings.

    D. 7 servings.

5. What is the recommended way to flavor popcorn as a high-fiber snack?

    A. Use oil and butter.

    B. Add salt and pepper.

    C. Use salt substitutes or herb mixtures.

    D. Eat it plain without any flavoring.

Unit 13
Algorithmic Bias

Activity Two

Listen to a lecture about how climate influences species diversity and fill in each blank within three words.

1. What is one noticeable difference between polar and tropical ecosystems?
   Answer: Tropical ecosystems are more _____ in terms of plant and animal species.

2. How do seasonal fluctuations in temperature affect animals in polar ecosystems?
   Answer: Seasonal fluctuations in temperature result in _____ in the availability of food in polar regions.

3. What is the feeding behavior of polar animals?
   Answer: Polar animals exhibit generalist feeding behavior, covering a wide territory in search for food and displaying _____ in their eating habits.

4. Could you provide an example of a generalist species in the polar ecosystem?
   Answer: The Arctic Fox is an example of a generalist species that mainly feeds on _____ but also includes migratory birds, their eggs, insects, berries, and scavenged prey.

5. How does temperature stability in the tropics impact animals' feeding behavior?
   Answer: With temperature stability, animals in tropical ecosystems don't have to constantly _____ their feeding behavior to changing conditions.

6. What is the feeding behavior of animals in tropical ecosystems?
   Answer: Animals in tropical ecosystems tend to be specialists, living in one specific part of the habitat and feeding on one _____ kind of food.

7. Could you provide an example of a specialist species in a tropical ecosystem?
   Answer: The Yellow Eared Parrot in Colombia is an example of a specialist species that nests in wax palm trees and mainly feeds on the _____ of the wax palm.

8. Why does specialization in food preference lead to more diversity in tropical ecosystems?
   Answer: Each species specializing in a particular type of food leads to the division of ecological resources, creating microhabitats that support unique species suited to _____ on specific food and living space conditions.

9. What advantage do generalist species have over specialists in terms of territory coverage?
   Answer: Generalist species cover a(n) _____ territory in search of food compared with specialists.

10. What is the downside of being a specialist species?

Answer: The downside of being a specialist species is the vulnerability to habitat loss. If the microhabitat, including the specific food source, disappears, the specialist species may starve and face the risk of _____ due to their dependence on a limited resource.

Activity Three

Listen to a passage about the engraved block printing craftsmanship and fill in each blank within three words.

Engraved Block Printing Craftsmanship

Engraved block printing, a printing technique originating in China, is regarded as a "living fossil" in the history of printing.

First of all, a piece of 1. _____ with characters written on it, is pasted on a block that is carefully sawed from wood, with the character covered side facing the block. Then following the strokes of each character, the background is 2. _____ away, leaving the strokes raised on the block. Coming to the printing process, first the engraved block needs to be brushed with 3. _____. Then cover it with a piece of blank paper and use a clean brush to slightly brush the 4. _____ of the paper. After that, take off the paper, and the page of a book is ready after all the pages are printed in this way, and 5. _____, a book is produced. Since the printing is carried out on an engraved wood block, the method is known as "engraved block printing".

Engraved block printing was created by ancient Chinese in the 6. _____ century. It liberated people from the onerous job of copying 7. _____. In the year 1041, Bi Sheng of the Northern Song Dynasty invented movable-type printing by using baked 8. _____ which greatly accelerated the speed of typesetting and printing.

All the revolutions in printing technology enhance 9. _____ development. Nowadays, printing has already entered the era of laser typesetting, but it doesn't erase the fact that block printing had played a significant role in 10. _____, recording histories and exchanging cultures for more than one thousand years.

Unit 14

Artificial Intelligence

Learning Objectives

In this unit, you will:

- learn about the advancement of AI;
- learn to guess the meaning of listening materials;
- learn to speak to demonstrate.

Background

AI is widely used in speech recognition, image recognition, natural language processing, smart robots, autonomous vehicles, and more. With the creation of powerful AI tools like ChatGPT, many people share concerns about the potential of AI technology to threaten jobs. However, it has many advantages, such as improved productivity, accurate disease diagnosis, personalized services, and improved quality of life. Many companies are trying to prevent its harm and make it beneficial to people's lives.

Section A Listening

Pre-Listening

Work in pairs and discuss the following questions.

1. Do you think that AI will impact the creative industry, such as music and art?
2. Will AI replace human creativity or enhance it?

Activity One

Work in small groups to find the best answer to each question.

1. Which of the following is TRUE about AI?

    A. It eliminates dull and boring tasks.

    B. It can imitate human cognition.

    C. It helps prevent natural disasters.

    D. All of the above.

2. What are some potential applications of generative AI?

    A. Financial analysis, supply chain optimization, and customer service.

    B. Natural language processing, computer vision, metaverse, and speech synthesis.

    C. Social media marketing, search engine optimization, and email automation.

    D. None of the above.

3. What is the risk associated with AI technology?

    A. The creation of deepfakes that aim to impersonate people.

B. The automation of jobs that require human skills.

C. The over-reliance on technology in decision-making.

D. All of the above.

4. How can generative AI technology be used to improve people's lives?

A. By automating as many tasks as possible.

B. By maximizing profits and gaining a competitive advantage.

C. By developing applications that prioritize human well-being and limit harm.

D. By eliminating the need for human decision-making.

5. What do you do with AI tools in your daily life? (You can choose more than one answer)

A. Language translation.

B. Speech recognition.

C. Digital assistants, like Siri.

D. Chatbots.

While-Listening

Text A　Risks from Advanced Artificial Intelligence

Language Bank

existential	[ˌegzɪˈstenʃl]	adj.	存在的
celebrity	[səˈlebrəti]	n.	名人
titan	[ˈtaɪtn]	n.	巨头
convergent	[kənˈvɜːdʒənt]	adj.	会聚性的
humanity	[hjuːˈmænəti]	n.	人道
ultimately	[ˈʌltɪmətli]	adv.	最后
hypothetical	[ˌhaɪpəˈθetɪkl]	adj.	假设的
counterargument	[ˈkaʊntərɑːgjumənt]	n.	抗辩
intrinsically	[ɪnˈtrɪnzɪkli]	adv.	本质地
high-profile	[ˌhaɪ ˈprəʊfaɪl]	adj.	备受瞩目的
militarized	[ˈmɪlɪtəraɪzd]	adj.	军事化的

Activity Two

You will hear a passage about risks caused by advanced artificial intelligence. Listen and choose the best answer to each question.

1. What does Nick Bostrom point out in his book *Superintelligence*?
   A. AI has a positive influence on the future development of humankind.
   B. AI has a creative effect on the high-tech science.
   C. AI will pose a threat to mankind.
   D. AI will produce a potential risk to commercial development.

2. According to Nick Bostrom, what will AI show if it chooses actions based on achieving some goals?
   A. It will exhibit positive behavior.
   B. It will show convergent behavior.
   C. It will protect itself from being opened up.
   D. It will protect itself from being started up.

3. If the existential danger is realized, what would the hypothetical AI do?
   A. It would have to overpower or out-think all of humanity.
   B. It would be an unworthy research.
   C. It would be developed within the power of humanity.
   D. It would not go far from the current level.

4. Which company is NOT mentioned funded by Musk to develop AI?
   A. Google.
   B. DeepMind.
   C. Baidu.
   D. Vicarious.

5. What is the related concern about AI?
   A. Developing militarized artificial intelligence.
   B. The development of battlefield robots.
   C. The development of super intelligent AI.
   D. Developing artificial soldiers.

Activity Three

Listen again and decide whether the following statements are true (T) or false (F).

( ) 1. A universal concern about the development of artificial intelligence is the existential threat that could pose to mankind.

( ) 2. A group of prominent tech titans has donated $1 billion to OpenAI.

( ) 3. Concern over risk from military artificial intelligence has led to some high-profile donations and investments.

( ) 4. In January 2015, Elon Musk donated 1,000,000 dollars to the Future of Life Institute to fund research on understanding AI decision-making.

( ) 5. Currently, more than 50 countries are researching battlefield robots, including China, the United States, the United Kingdom, and Russia.

Text B Unlocking the Potential of Generative AI

Language Bank

generative	['dʒenərətɪv]	adj.	能够自主生成新内容的
metaverse	['metəvɜːs]	n.	元宇宙
synthesis	['sɪnθəsɪs]	n.	合成，综合
deepfake	[diːpfeɪk]	n.	深度伪造
distinguish	[dɪ'stɪŋgwɪʃ]	v.	区分，辨别
simulator	['sɪmjuleɪtə(r)]	n	模拟器
validation	[ˌvælɪ'deɪʃn]	n.	验证
render	['rendə(r)]	v.	渲染
workflow	['wɜːkfləʊ]	n.	工作流

Activity Four

You will hear a passage about unlocking the potential of generative AI. Listen and decide whether the following statements are true (T) or false (F).

( ) 1. ChatGPT and DALL·E 2 are examples of generative AI tools.

( ) 2. Intel's Trusted Media team is working on generative AI applications with the goal of improving people's lives.

( ) 3. Intel's deepfake detection algorithms have a 100% accuracy rate.

(　　) 4. The speech synthesis project by Intel's Trusted Media team is being used to help individuals who have lost their voices communicate again.

(　　) 5. The Trusted Media research team is also working on using generative AI to make 4D experiences more realistic.

Activity Five

You will hear one part of the passage in Activity Four again. Listen and fill in each blank within three words.

Unlocking the Potential of Generative AI

I. Preventing Harm

◆ In the past few years, generative AI has become more powerful—and therefore more capable of doing 1. _____ in a more convincing and realistic manner. For example, generative models for 2. _____ aim to impersonate people. We defend against this in two ways.

◆ The first is with our deepfake detection 3. _____ integrated into our real-time platform. FakeCatcher, the core of the system, can detect fake videos with a 96% accuracy rate, enabling users to distinguish between real and fake content in 4. _____. The second is through our 5. _____, one of which makes human puzzles. As opposed to 6. _____ by training on real people's faces, this generator mixes and matches regions (nose of person A, mouth of person B, eyes of person C, etc.) to create an entirely new face that does not already exist in 7. _____.

II. Enhancing Lives

◆ To fulfill this vision, the team's 8. _____ project aims to enable people who have lost their voices to talk again. This technology is used in Intel's I Will Always Be Me digital storybook project in partnership with Dell Technologies, Rolls-Royce and the Motor Neuron Disease (MND) Association. The interactive website allows anyone 9. _____ with MND or any disease expected to affect their speaking ability to record their voice to be used on a(n) 10. _____.

Post-Listening

Work in pairs and discuss the following questions.

1. What are some potential risks and ethical considerations associated with the use of AI?

2. How might AI be used to create more inclusive and diverse representations in media and entertainment?

Section B Public Speaking

Activity One

Read the passage below and get some knowledge about speaking to demonstrate.

Speaking to Demonstrate

Speaking to demonstrate is a type of public speaking that aims to teach the audience how to do a particular thing. It is a clear, step-by-step practical guide that intends to show people methods of using regular items and even improve someone's life with it. It is a form of public speech that relies on visual aids and demonstrations to explain a process or a skill.

Speaking to demonstrate requires some skills and strategies, such as:
- choosing a topic that is suitable for your audience, setting, and time limit;
- breaking down the process or skill into simple and logical steps;
- preparing the necessary materials, equipment, and visual aids;
- practicing your speech and your demonstration beforehand;
- explaining each step clearly and concisely, using transitions and signposts;
- showing each step visually and verbally, using gestures, movements, and examples;
- checking for understanding and feedback from your audience;
- summarizing your main points and giving a call to action.

Activity Two

Answer the following questions according to the passage above.
1. What is the aim of demonstrative speaking?
2. What does demonstrate speaking rely on?
3. What are some traits of a good demonstrative speech?

Activity Three

Read one example of a demonstrative speech and complete the outline of it.

How to Do a Magic Trick

Hello everyone, I'm David Blaine and I'm here to show you how to do a magic trick. Magic is an art of illusion and deception that can amaze and entertain people. Magic tricks can be simple or complex, but they all rely on some basic principles and techniques. Today, I'm going to teach you how to do a card trick that you can perform anytime, anywhere, with any deck of cards. It's called the Rising Card Trick, and it will make a card that your spectator chooses rise out of the deck by itself. Here's how it works.

First, you need a deck of cards. You can use any deck you want, as long as it's not too old or worn out. You also need to prepare the deck before you perform the trick. To do this, you need to bend the cards slightly in the middle, so that they form a slight arch. This will create some tension in the cards that will help you later. You can bend the cards by holding them in your hands and gently pushing them together. Don't bend them too much or they will look suspicious. Just enough to create a subtle curve.

Next, you need to shuffle the cards and let your spectator choose one. You can shuffle the cards any way you like, as long as you don't disturb the bend in the cards. You can also let your spectator shuffle the cards if they want to. Then, spread the cards face down on the table and ask your spectator to pick one card and look at it. Don't let them show it to you or anyone else. Tell them to remember their card and put it back anywhere in the deck.

Now, you need to cut the deck and place it back on the table. To do this, you need to use a special technique called the jog shuffle. This will allow you to secretly mark where your spectator's card is in the deck. Here's how you do it. Hold the deck in your right hand and use your left thumb to lift about half of the cards from the bottom. As you do this, use your right pinky finger to pull back slightly on the bottom card of the top half. This will create a small gap or jog between the two halves of the deck. Then, place the bottom half on top of the top half, but don't align them perfectly. Leave a small step or ledge between them, so that you can see where the jog is.

Next, you need to cut the deck again and place it back on the table. This time, you need to cut at the jog, so that your spectator's card is on top of the bottom half of the deck. To do this, hold the deck in your right hand and use your left thumb to lift off all the cards above the jog. Then, place them on top of the remaining cards, but don't square them up yet. Leave a small step or ledge between them again, so that you can see where your spectator's card is.

Now, you need to square up the deck and place it back on the table. To do this, hold the deck in your right hand and use your left hand to push all the cards together from both sides. As you do this, use your right thumb to push down slightly on your spectator's card, so that it sticks out a little bit from the back of the deck. This will create a small break or gap between your spectator's card and the rest of the cards. Then, place the deck face down on the table and make sure that no one can see the break or gap.

Now comes the fun part. You need to make your spectator's card rise out of the deck by itself. To do this, you need to use your index finger to secretly lift up their card from behind. Here's how you do it. Hold your right hand above the deck and pretend that you are going to wave it over the cards or snap your fingers. As you do this, move your hand behind the deck and use your index finger to hook into the break or gap that you created earlier. Then, slowly pull up their card with your finger until it rises above the rest of the cards. Make sure that no one can see your finger behind the deck.

And that's it! You've just done a magic trick by David Blaine. Show your spectator their card and watch their reaction. They will be amazed and impressed by your skills. You can also repeat the trick with different cards or spectators, as long as you prepare the deck and create the break or gap each time. Thank you for watching and have a magical day!

	How to Do a Magic Trick
Introduction	• Explanation of magic as an art of illusion and deception • Overview of the Rising Card Trick
Preparation	• Selecting a suitable 1. _____ • Bending the cards slightly to create tension
Performance	• Shuffling the deck without 2. _____ the bend • Spectator selects a card and remembers it • Card is returned to the 3. _____ • Using the jog shuffle technique to secretly mark the card's position • Cutting the deck to place the spectator's card on top of the 4. _____ half • Squaring up the deck with a small break or gap behind the card • The spectator's card rises out of the deck
Conclusion	• Recap of the trick's steps • Encouragement to practice and perform the trick with different 5. _____ and spectators • Thanking the audience for watching

Activity Four

Choose one of the following topics and deliver a demonstrative speech about technology with the help of the public speaking skill above.

◆ How to use a specific software or app

◆ How to build a simple website or blog

◆ How to use AI or machine learning for a specific task

Section C Further Listening

Activity One

You will hear a university lecturer giving a talk to a group of students about the role of motivation in foreign language learning. Listen and choose the best answer to each question.

1. What is integrative motivation based on?

    A. External incentives and rewards.

    B. Personal interest in the people and culture of the language group.

    C. Improving social status and meeting educational requirements.

    D. Achieving goals of integrating with the target language community.

2. Which type of motivation is driven by external incentives?

    A. Instrumental motivation.

    B. Intrinsic motivation.

    C. Integrative motivation.

    D. Extrinsic motivation.

3. Intrinsic motivation occurs when a person is rewarded by _____.

    A. achieving personal goals

    B. interacting with the target language community

    C. participating in the activity itself

    D. meeting educational requirements

4. What has recent research found about integrative motivation in formal learning contexts?

    A. It is positively correlated with achievement measures.

    B. It is more powerful than instrumental orientation.

C. It is influenced by situational factors.

D. It is not relevant in foreign language learning.

5. What distinguishes the motivation of foreign language learners from second language learners?

    A. Foreign language learners have less exposure to the target language community.

    B. Second language learners have a stronger integrative orientation.

    C. Foreign language learners are more intrinsically motivated.

    D. Second language learners don't communicate on a day-to-day basis in the target language.

6. Which factor may have an important part to play in foreign language learning, particularly for international languages like English?

    A. Instrumental motivation.

    B. Sociocultural motivation.

    C. Intellectual motivation.

    D. All of the above.

7. What are some additional reasons for Japanese learners to learn English, according to researchers?

    A. Meeting educational requirements and improving social status.

    B. Integrating with the target language community.

    C. Pleasure at being able to read English and enjoyment of entertainment in English.

    D. Compulsory nature of English learning in Japan.

8. Why might some students in Japan respond more to situational factors than personal reasons for learning English?

    A. Lack of integrative motivation.

    B. Compulsory nature of English learning.

    C. Limited exposure to the target language community.

    D. Instrumental motivation.

9. What does the complexity of motivation depend on in foreign language learning?

    A. The country in which learners live.

    B. The language learners are studying.

    C. Personal and affective factors unique to individual learners.

    D. All of the above.

10. According to the lecture, what should instructors consider in applying research on motivation in foreign language learning?
   A. The types of motivation applicable to specific learners.
   B. The cultural background of the learners.
   C. The impact of situational factors on motivation.
   D. The role of instrumental motivation in achieving goals.

 **Activity Two**

Listen to part of a lecture in an education class. Complete the outline by filling in each blank within three words.

Musical Ability and Development in Children

I. Introduction

All children are born with some innate skill for musical development.

Even newborns are sensitive to 1. _____.

II. Early Musical Development in Children

Babies respond actively to music at a very young age.
- At 2. _____, children begin engaging in spontaneous singing.
- Spontaneous songs start disappearing as children start 3. _____ the learned songs.

III. Importance of Early Exposure to Music

Children need to understand the 4. _____ between certain kinds of music and certain moods/events in their culture.

Early exposure to music brings 5. _____.

IV. Formal Music Instruction

In Western cultures, musical ability reaches a developmental plateau at age 6. _____ without formal training.

Research suggests a small window of 7. _____ when children can be trained to play music at a high level.

Musical education is 8. _____ for developing musical ability and appreciation.

V. Conclusion

9. _____ to music is important for children's development.

10. _____ music instruction can help develop musical ability and appreciation in children.

Unit 14
Artificial Intelligence

Activity Three

Listen to a passage about the Chinese traditional architectural craftsmanship for timber-framed structures and fill in each blank within three words.

Chinese Traditional Architectural Craftsmanship for Timber-Framed Structures

The traditional Chinese architecture craftsmanship for timber-framed structures has its own unique system of characteristics through thousands of years of development, with so much rich experience accumulated over time.

Chinese craftsmen have developed very 1. _____ technical methods, regarding the choice of building materials, types of framework, manufacturing of components installation and so on, which have been 2. _____ from masters to their apprentices. Through examples and verbal instructions by employing the architectural craftsmanship, various kinds of architectures such as 3. _____, temples, 4. _____, residential houses and assembly halls, cater to the needs of people from all walks of life, reflect Chinese people's view of the 5. _____, the traditional Chinese hierarchy society as well as 6. _____ and demonstrate the wisdom of ancient technology. Not only are they the 7. _____ of Chinese people's unique aesthetics, but also representatives of ancient oriental architectural technology.

Timber-frame is the 8. _____ of the structure. There are mainly two types of framework for traditional Chinese timber structures—one post and lintel and the other column and tie beam. The framework consists of wooden components including 9. _____, beams, purlins rafters and bracket sets. Generally known as structural frame, the tenon joints connecting the wooden components contribute to the 10. _____ of the structure, which makes it more earthquake-resistant.

Unit 15
ChatGPT

Learning Objectives

In this unit, you will:
- learn about ChatGPT;
- learn to listen for main ideas;
- learn to speak in competitions.

Background

Today ChatGPT is popular in every country. There has been a lot of interest in the chatbot developed by OpenAI. Do you know how ChatGPT works? Can we trust what it tells us in a conversation?

Section A Listening

Pre-Listening

Work in pairs and discuss the following questions.
1. What is ChatGPT?
2. How does ChatGPT work?

Activity One

Complete the sentences by choosing the correct words and filling in each blank. Change the form of the words where necessary.

1. We've trained a model called ChatGPT, which _____ in a(n) _____ way.
   (connect/conversational/interact/conversant/communicate)

2. _____ by artificial intelligence and machine learning, ChatGPT can _____ information and answer questions through a conversation.
   (push/train/provide/give/get)

3. Chatbots can make it _____ for users to find the information they need by responding to their questions and requests—through text input, audio input, or both—without the need for human _____.
   (easy/hard/frequent/ intervention/participation)

Unit 15 ChatGPT

🎧 While-Listening

Text A   An Introduction to ChatGPT

📞 Language Bank

conversational	[ˌkɒnvə'seɪʃənl]	adj.	健谈的
scrub	[skrʌb]	v.	搜索、搜查
gauge	[geɪdʒ]	v.	评估、判断
brainchild	['breɪntʃaɪld]	n.	独创的点子
sophisticated	[sə'fɪstɪkeɪtɪd]	adj.	聪明世俗的
snippet	['snɪpɪt]	n.	片段
component	[kəm'pəʊnənt]	n.	组成部分
convert	['kɒnvɜːt]	v.	转变、改造
plausible-sounding	['plɔːzəbl 'saʊndɪŋ]	adj.	听上去合理的

🎧 Activity Two

You will hear an introduction to ChatGPT. Listen and choose the best answer to each question.

1. The following can all be used to describe ChatGPT EXCEPT _____.
   A. ChatGPT scrubs the Internet for potential answers
   B. ChatGPT delivers unique and novel answers never written by humans before
   C. ChatGPT is used to help customers get what they need
   D. ChaGPT can tackle the "Imitation Game" that computer scientist Alan Turing proposed in 1950

2. What is the writer suggesting about chatbots?
   A. Companies have successfully used chatbots instead of humans to handle customer service work.
   B. Ujet's study showed more than half of the people think chatbots are a waste of time.
   C. People can ask anything and get an answer from chatbots.
   D. ChatGPT has rapidly become a widely used tool on- and off-line.

3. According to the passage, what can chatbots do?
   ① To develop a "safe and beneficial" artificial general intelligence system.
   ② To generate texts as humans can do.

③ To create "generative art" based on text prompts people type in.

A. ①②
B. ②③
C. ①③
D. ①②③

4. Which of the following is NOT true about ChatGPT?

   A. There are three language models mentioned in the passage.

   B. ChatGPT can be trained automatically to create text based on what they've seen.

   C. Some people are hired by OpenAI to review thousands of snippets of text for problems like violence, sexual abuse, and hate speech.

   D. ChatGPT searches relevant information and converts that into plausible-sounding texts.

5. What is the passage mainly about?

   A. OpenAI.

   B. ChatGPT.

   C. AI technology.

   D. Language models.

Activity Three

Listen to the introduction again and complete the answers to the questions by filling in each blank within three words.

1. What is ChatGPT?

   Answer: ChatGPT is an AI chatbot that uses available data found online to give users 1. _____ to a host of questions and give people 2. _____ that they themselves must read.

2. What is "Imitation Game"?

   Answer: It's a test proposed by a computer scientist Alan Turing as a way to gauge 3. _____: Can a human conversing with a human and with a computer tell 4. _____?

3. What categories are suggested by OpenAI?

   Answer: OpenAI suggests a few categories, like explaining 5. _____, asking for birthday party ideas and getting 6. _____.

4. How do large language models work?

   Answer: The training process can find a(n) 7. _____ paragraph of text, delete a few words, ask the AI to fill in the blanks, and compare the result with the original. Repeating over and over can lead to a sophisticated ability to 8. _____.

5. What are the defects of ChatGPT?

   Answer: It's not totally automated and it needs to be evaluated and 9. _____ by humans. In fact, ChatGPT doesn't actually 10. _____ the way you do.

Text B The Limits and Off Limits of ChatGPT

Language Bank

stab	[stæb]	n.	尝试
sandwich	['sænwɪtʃ]	v.	夹在……中间
authoritative	[ɔː'θɒrətətɪv]	adj.	权威的
articulate	[ɑː'tɪkjuleɪt]	v.	明确表达
altered	['ɔːltə(r)d]	adj.	改变的
weed	[wiːd]	v.	清除
discriminatory	[dɪ'skrɪmɪnətəri]	adj.	不公平的

Activity Four

You will hear a passage about the limits and off limits of ChatGPT. Listen and fill in each blank within three words.

What Are the Limits and Off Limits of ChatGPT?

I. What are the limits of ChatGPT?

◆ ChatGPT can give you 1. _____ and "a misleading impression of greatness".

◆ It is hard for ChatGPT to judge without 2. _____ and it will just show one possible interpretation when it takes a stab at the meaning of an expression.

◆ ChatGPT's answers can look 3. _____ but be wrong.

◆ ChatGPT may constitute 4. _____ no different from altered images or plagiarism of existing works.

◆ The 5. _____ of getting correct answers from ChatGPT is too low.

II. What are the off limits of ChatGPT?

◆ ChatGPT is designed to weed out inappropriate requests to ensure that artificial

general intelligence benefits 6. _____.
- Discriminatory, offensive, or 7. _____, including the ones that are racist, sexist, or otherwise discriminatory or 8. _____.
- Asking ChatGPT to engage in 9. _____.
- Using for 10. _____—write phishing emails to try to fool people into parting with sensitive information.

Activity Five

Listen again and decide whether the following statements are true (T) or false (F).

(   ) 1. ChatGPT is able to browse the Internet or access any external information beyond what it was trained on.
(   ) 2. People can always get the right answer no matter what questions they ask.
(   ) 3. A software developer site banned ChatGPT answers to programming questions.
(   ) 4. ChatGPT is a notable development in computing.
(   ) 5. ChatGPT is designed to get rid of "inappropriate" requests and to ensure that it benefits all of humanity.

Post-Listening

Work in pairs and discuss the following questions.
1. What do you think of ChatGPT?
2. How can you make use of ChatGPT in the correct way?

Section B Public Speaking

Activity One

Read the passage below and get some knowledge about speaking in competitions.

Speaking in Competitions

Speaking in competitions is a type of public speech that aims to win a contest or a prize by impressing the judges and the audience with your skills and abilities. It is a challenging and rewarding way to showcase your talent, knowledge, and personality. The common types of speaking in competitions are the following:

Debate

A formal discussion on a specific topic where two or more teams present opposing arguments and try to persuade the judges and the audience to support their position.

Oratory

A speech that expresses a personal opinion or viewpoint on a significant issue or theme using logic, emotion, and rhetoric.

Poetry

A performance of a poem or a selection of poems that conveys the meaning, mood, and tone of the text using voice, gestures, and facial expressions.

Prose

A performance of a short story or a selection of stories that conveys the plot, characters, and theme of the text using voice, gestures, and facial expressions.

Storytelling

A performance of a folk tale or a personal narrative that engages the audience with humor, suspense, and emotion using voice, gestures, and facial expressions.

Activity Two

Answer the following questions according to the passage above.

1. What is the aim of speaking in competitions?
2. What does speaking in competitions showcase?
3. How many types of speaking in competitions are there? What are they?

Activity Three

Read one example of a speech and complete the outline of it.

How to Be a Champion

Hello everyone, I'm Serena Williams and I'm here to talk to you about how to be a champion. Champion is not just a title or a trophy. It's a mindset, an attitude, and a way of life. It's something that you have to work for every day, no matter what challenges you face or what obstacles you encounter. It's something that you have to earn, not just once, but over and over again. Today, I'm going to share with you some of the lessons that I've learned from my journey as a champion, and how you can apply them to your own goals and dreams.

First, you have to believe in yourself. You have to have confidence in your abilities and your potential. You have to trust that you have what it takes to succeed, even when others doubt you or criticize you. You have to be your own biggest fan and your own best coach. You have to tell yourself that you can do it, that you are capable, that you are worthy. You have to visualize yourself achieving your goals and celebrating your victories. You have to affirm yourself with positive words and thoughts every day.

Second, you have to work hard. You have to put in the time, the effort, and the dedication to improve your skills and your performance. You have to practice, train, study, and learn from your mistakes. You have to push yourself beyond your comfort zone and challenge yourself to do better than before. You have to set high standards for yourself and strive to meet them or exceed them. You have to be disciplined, consistent, and persistent. You have to work hard when no one is watching and when no one is cheering.

Third, you have to be passionate. You have to love what you do and do what you love. You have to enjoy the process and the journey, not just the outcome and the destination. You have to find joy and satisfaction in your work and your achievements. You have to be motivated by your own inner drive and desire, not by external rewards or recognition. You have to be passionate about your purpose and your mission, not just your profession and your career.

Fourth, you have to be resilient. You have to overcome adversity and bounce back from setbacks. You have to face your fears and conquer your doubts. You have to deal with pressure and stress with grace and poise. You have to cope with pain and injury with courage and strength. You have to handle failure and loss with humility and dignity. You have to learn from every experience and grow from every challenge. You have to be resilient in the face of hardship and difficulty.

Fifth, you have to be grateful. You have to appreciate what you have and what you've achieved. You have to acknowledge the people who helped you along the way and the opportunities that opened up for you. You have to express your gratitude for the support and encouragement that you received from your family, friends, coaches, mentors, fans, and sponsors. You have to give back to the community and the society that gave you so much. You have to be grateful for the privilege and the honor of being a champion.

And finally, you have to be humble. You have to remember where you came from and who you are. You have to respect your opponents and your competitors. You have to honor the game and the sport that you play. You have to share your success and your glory with others. You have to inspire others with your example and your story. You have to be humble in the midst of fame and fortune.

These are some of the lessons that I've learned from being a champion. And I hope that they can help you achieve your own goals and dreams. Because being a champion is not just about winning trophies or medals. It's about being the best version of yourself that you can be. It's about being a champion in life.

Thank you for listening.

	How to Be a Champion
Introduction	A. Introduction of the speaker (Serena Williams) and the topic of becoming a champion B. Explanation that being a champion is more than just a title or a(n) 1. _____
Body	A. Believing in yourself • Importance of self-belief and confidence • Overcoming doubt and criticism • Visualization and positive affirmations B. Working hard • The value of effort and 2. _____ • Continuous improvement and learning from mistakes • Pushing beyond comfort zones and setting high standards C. Being passionate • Finding joy and fulfillment in one's pursuits • Intrinsic motivation and inner 3. _____ D. Being resilient • Overcoming adversity and setbacks • Dealing with pressure and stress • Learning from experiences and growing from challenges E. Being grateful • Appreciating one's achievements and support system • Giving back to the community • 4. _____ gratitude and humility F. Being humble • Respecting opponents and competitors • Honoring the sport and the game • Inspiring others and sharing 5. _____
Conclusion	A. Recap of the lessons for becoming a champion B. Encouragement to apply the lessons to personal goals and dreams C. Thanking the audience and expressing blessings

Activity Four

Choose one of the following topics and deliver a speech related to programming with the help of the public speaking skill above.

- The power of Algorithms
- Mastering data structures
- Dynamic programming demystified

Section C Further Listening

Activity One

You will hear a talk in a psychology class. Listen and choose the best answer to each question.

1. What is prosody in language?

   A. The ability to control pitch and volume of sounds.

   B. The elements of language that contribute to its acoustic and rhythmic effects.

   C. The process of learning language perception.

   D. The recognition of specific vowel sounds.

2. What have studies shown about infants' recognition of prosodic features?

   A. Infants can recognize prosodic features as soon as they are born.

   B. Infants can recognize prosodic features at around three months of age.

   C. Infants cannot recognize prosodic features until they start speaking.

   D. Infants have no control over prosodic patterns.

3. When do babies typically start producing specific vowel sounds that match their native language?

   A. Around three months of age.

   B. Before birth.

   C. As soon as they are born.

   D. After six months of age.

4. Why have infants younger than three months not been studied regarding their production of sounds matching their native language?

   A. They do not have control over the necessary muscles for sound production.

B. Their cries are not considered a form of language production.

C. They have not been exposed to enough language input.

D. They are not capable of imitating prosodic patterns.

5. What did the analysis of newborns' cries from different language households reveal?

    A. The cries are solely determined by the amount of air in the lungs.

    B. The cries match the specific intonation patterns of the language spoken in the household.

    C. The cries have no correlation with the language spoken in the household.

    D. The cries follow a universal pattern across all languages.

6. What did the researchers conclude about newborns' ability to control pitch and volume in their cries?

    A. Newborns have no control over the pitch and volume of their cries.

    B. Newborns can only imitate the prosody of their native language when speaking.

    C. Newborns have the ability to independently control the pitch and volume of their cries.

    D. Newborns can imitate prosody, but only after a few months of exposure to their native language.

7. In which language would it be interesting to study the cry patterns of newborns?

    A. Chinese.

    B. African language.

    C. English.

    D. Japanese.

8. According to the information provided, where does at least some learning of language prosody likely occur?

    A. In the first hours and days of life.

    B. In the last few months in the womb.

    C. After three months of age.

    D. After exposure to the target language community.

9. What can be concluded about the learning process of fetuses in the womb?

    A. They learn the prosody of their native language but cannot reproduce it after birth.

    B. They learn the prosody of their native language and can reproduce aspects of it after birth.

    C. They cannot learn language before birth.

    D. Their language learning begins only after birth.

10. What is the main focus of the studies mentioned in the lecture?

   A. The recognition of specific vowel sounds in newborns.

   B. The role of language perception in language learning.

   C. The ability of newborns to control the pitch and volume of their cries.

   D. The learning of prosodic features by fetuses in the womb.

 **Activity Two**

Listen to a lecture in an archaeology class and complete the outline by filling in each blank within three words.

Cave Paintings

I. Introduction

- Cave paintings in France around 31,000 years ago
- Depictions of 1. _____ (bulls, horses, deer) and their lifelike nature

II. Uncovering the Significance of Accompanying Markings

- Researcher Genevie Vampithinger's 2. _____ study of the markings
- Compilation of a database of 3. _____ repeated signs or symbols

III. Exploring the Potential Symbolism and Writing Code

- 4. _____ between realistic paintings and symbolic markings
- Examining the possibility of a writing-like system
- 5. _____ of style among the signs

IV. Synecdoche and the Representation of Ideas

- Synecdoche as a feature of 6. _____ writing systems
- Example of oval eyes representing whole animal figures
- Indication of symbolic 7. _____ of ideas

V. Combination of Symbols and a Fully Formed System

- Pairing of symbols to create new 8. _____
- Presence of signs in the oldest cave sites without 9. _____ of development
- Speculation on the signs being brought from 10. _____ by early migrants

Unit 15
ChatGPT

Activity Three

You will hear a passage about how China enhances its sci-tech and innovation capacity. Listen and match the organization with the measures it is going to take.

1. High-quality research universities	A. Integrating science, talent, and innovation
2. Leading science and technology enterprises	B. Driving industrial and economic development
	C. Cultivating more outstanding talent
3. Provincial governments	D. Applying and commercializing scientific and technological advances
	E. Building national or regional sci-tech innovation centers

Unit 16
Digital Darwinism

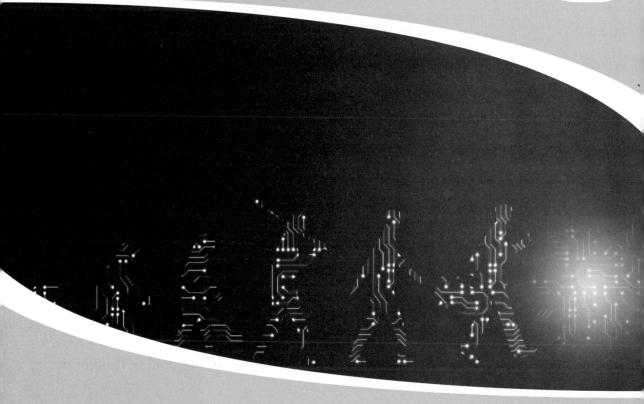

Learning Objectives

In this unit, you will:
- learn about basic knowledge of Digital Darwinism;
- learn to listen for implied meanings;
- learn to speak on special occasions.

Background

Digital Darwinism is the application of Darwin's theory of evolution to the digital economy, where an organization's success or failure to adopt technology directly affects its survival as a business. The phrase was coined by Evan I. Schwartz in 1999 in reference to an era where technology and society are evolving faster than businesses can naturally adapt. Today the phrase has been popularized by digital analyst Brian Solis. In 2011, Solis wrote in *The Washington Post*: "Digital Darwinism is the evolution of consumer behavior when society and technology evolve faster than some companies' ability to adapt. The point of natural selection is that only some businesses will survive."

Section A Listening

Pre-Listening

Work in pairs and discuss the following questions.

1. Why does Digital Darwinism appear?
2. How is Digital Darwinism different from Darwinism?

Activity One

Complete the sentence by choosing the proper words and putting them in the correct order.

1. _____ _____ _____ _____ is vital to obtain a competitive advantage and to survive in the age of digital Darwinism.
   (swift/change/adaptation/to)
2. Surviving in the new age necessarily means _____ _____ _____ of the company.
   (transformation/digital/following)
3. New technologies will be the _____ _____ _____ _____ and will impact production models, manpower, relationships with consumers, etc.
   (cornerstones/transformation/this/of)

Unit 16 Digital Darwinism

While-Listening

Text A The Age of Digital Darwinism

Language Bank

divine	[dɪ'vaɪn]	adj.	绝妙的
metabolic	[ˌmetə'bɒlɪk]	adj.	变化的
penetration	[ˌpenə'treɪʃn]	n.	渗透，穿透
compound	['kɒmpaʊnd]	v.	加重
accrue	[ə'kruː]	vi.	积累
linear	['lɪniə(r)]	adj.	直线的
exponential	[ˌekspə'nenʃl]	adj.	越来越快的
agile	['ædʒaɪl]	adj.	轻快的

Activity Two

You will hear an introduction to Digital Darwinism. Listen and choose the best answer to each question.

1. The following can all be used to describe the theory of evolution EXCEPT _____.
   A. it was proposed in 1859
   B. it suggests that insects, animals, and humans are stages of a process
   C. Darwin argued that species advance through natural selection and competition
   D. it is no longer applied broadly today

2. What has changed in the age of Digital Darwinism?
   ① The development of new technologies makes the barriers of a business become lower.
   ② Companies with the digital capabilities get more benefits.
   ③ The advances in technology have intensified the competition.
   ④ The businesses that survive are the strongest or most intelligent.
   A. ①②③
   B. ①②④
   C. ①③④
   D. ②③④

3. Which of the following is true about the changes that happen in the age of Darwinism?

   A. The disruption is limited to the technology field.

   B. According to the survey, few businesses are experiencing digital disruption.

   C. These changes will force companies, industries, and entire countries to adapt to increased competition.

   D. Only companies will be influenced by changes in the tech sector.

4. All of the following have been mentioned in the passage EXCEPT _____.

   A. the successful ones will evolve and build stronger systems

   B. the successful ones accrue advantages in a linear pattern

   C. with more than 60% of the world connected to the Internet, innovation can spread across the world at a breakneck speed

   D. in a networked global economy, growth is exponential

5. What is the passage mainly about?

   A. The theory of evolution.

   B. New technologies.

   C. Digital Darwinism.

   D. The growth of global economy.

Activity Three

Listen again and decide whether the following statements are true (T) or false (F).

(   ) 1. Powerful new technologies can be applied by companies across different industries.

(   ) 2. Big corporations will lose because a small business with a big idea can scale it quickly with digital technologies.

(   ) 3. The penetration of e-commerce in the US benefited companies with the digital capabilities to service customers offline.

(   ) 4. Successful companies, industries or countries will develop into more agile and efficient organisms.

(   ) 5. Digital Darwinism shows us the possibility of rapid growth, and we will be sure to end up on the right side of disruption.

Unit 16
Digital Darwinism

Text B Tendency Under the Digital Darwinism

Language Bank

enthusiast	[ɪn'θjuːziæst]	n.	爱好者
continuous	[kən'tɪnjuəs]	adj.	连续的
Bogota	[bəʊɡə'ta]	n.	波哥大
Munich	['mjuːnik]	n.	慕尼黑
Seoul	[səʊl]	n.	首尔
Sao Paulo			圣保罗

Activity Four

You will hear a passage about the tendency under Digital Darwinism. Listen and fill in each blank within three words.

What Is the Tendency Under Digital Darwinism?

As the physical event literally moved across the globe, digital media enthusiasts 1. _____ its progress live online. As Hidalgo noted, our revenue went up and it presented how we could combine consumers' 2. _____ experiences to make a more powerful linkage.

Place context 3. _____ content. The distribution of their timing, context and 4. _____ is very important. 5. _____, marketers tend to raise the profile of media strategy and plan within their organizations. Marketers begin to shift their 6. _____ strategies to build capabilities in communication planning.

7. _____ one-fifth of the marketers in our study have invested in internal communication planning functions. Media agencies that plan and 8. _____ the marketers' media buys are becoming important partners with them.

Associated with this major point on the media mix is the demand for greater 9. _____ _____ and speed. In fact, most marketers say that media will be bought and sold in real-time, 10. _____ and continuous basis.

Activity Five

You will continue to listen to the passage and answer the following questions by filling in each blank within three words.

1. What is the major obstacle to the whole ecosystem's transition to a new marketing and media model?

Answer: _____ reliable and standard metrics.

2. Why do leading marketers build relationships with digital agencies and other media companies?
   Answer: In order to track ad placement, versioning, and _____.

3. What helps marketers assess the total return on their expenditure in MTV?
   Answer: A proprietary planning tool called _____.

4. What has the linear value chain been replaced with?
   Answer: It has been replaced with a vast, _____ of brands, consumers and media.

5. Which kind of companies carry a decided advantage?
   Answer: Those companies that convert through conversation, that collaborate in executing and measuring what matters, and that _____ as much as the message carry a decided advantage.

Post-Listening

Work in pairs and discuss the following questions.
1. Does it make any sense for companies struggling to transform their business models? Why or why not?
2. Is it useful for companies to cooperate with other media companies? Why or why not?

Section B Public Speaking

Read the passage below and get some knowledge about speaking on special occasions.

Speaking on Special Occasions

Speaking on special occasions is a type of speech that is given to mark the significance of a particular event or celebrate a person or a group. Special occasion speeches can be informative, persuasive, entertaining, or inspirational, depending on the purpose and the audience.

Some common types of special occasion speeches are:

Introduction

A speech that introduces another speaker and his or her speech to the audience.

Presentation

A speech that presents an award, a gift, or a recognition to someone or a group.

Acceptance

A speech that expresses gratitude and appreciation for receiving an award, a gift, or a recognition from someone or a group.

Dedication

A speech that honors or commemorates a person, a place, or an object that has special significance or value.

Toast

A speech that expresses good wishes or congratulations to someone or a group on a happy occasion, such as a wedding, a birthday, or an anniversary.

Roast

A speech that humorously teases or mocks someone or a group in a friendly and respectful way.

Eulogy

A speech that pays tribute to someone who has died by highlighting his or her achievements, qualities, and contributions.

Farewell

A speech that bids goodbye to someone or a group who is leaving or retiring.

Activity Two

Answer the following questions according to the passage above.

1. What is the aim of speaking on special occasions?
2. What are the common types of special occasions?
3. What is a eulogy speech for?

Activity Three

Read one example of a farewell speech and complete the outline of it.

How to Say Goodbye to Hollywood

Hello everyone, I'm Daniel Day-Lewis and I'm here to say goodbye to Hollywood. Yes, you heard me right. I'm retiring from acting after a long and rewarding career. I know this may come as a shock to some of you, but I hope you'll understand and respect my decision. Today, I want to share with you some of the reasons why I'm leaving this profession, and some of the memories that I'll cherish forever.

First of all, let me say that I love acting. I love the craft, the art, the challenge, the joy of creating characters and bringing them to life on screen. I love working with talented directors, writers, producers, and fellow actors who inspire me and push me to do my best. I love the connection that I have with the audience, who watch my films and appreciate my work. Acting has been my passion and my calling since I was a boy, and I'm grateful for every opportunity that I've had to pursue it.

However, acting has also been a demanding and exhausting profession. It requires a lot of dedication, discipline, sacrifice, and commitment. It takes a toll on your physical, mental, and emotional health. It affects your personal life, your relationships, your privacy, your identity. It consumes you completely, sometimes to the point where you lose yourself in the process. For me, acting has always been more than a job. It's been a way of life. And as much as I love it, I feel that it's time for me to move on to a different way of life.

I've always been selective about the roles that I choose and the projects that I work on. I've always tried to challenge myself and to do justice to the characters that I play. I've always given everything that I have to each performance, sometimes at the expense of my own well-being. And I've always felt that each film that I make could be my last one. That's why I've decided to end my career on a high note, with a film that I'm very proud of and that means a lot to me: *Phantom Thread*, directed by Paul Thomas Anderson.

Phantom Thread is a film about a fashion designer in 1950s London who falls in love with a young woman who becomes his muse and his partner. It's a film about creativity, obsession, passion, and love. It's a film that explores the complex and mysterious relationship between an artist and his work. It's a film that reflects some of my own experiences and feelings as an actor. And it's a film that marks the end of an era for me.

Working on *Phantom Thread* was one of the most rewarding and fulfilling experiences of my career. It was also one of the most difficult and draining ones. It took a lot out of me, physically and emotionally. It made me realize that I don't have the same energy or enthusiasm or desire that I used to have for acting. It made me realize that I need a change. A change of pace, a change of scenery, a change of direction. A change that will allow me to explore other aspects of myself and other interests that I have outside of acting.

That's why I'm retiring from acting. Not because I don't love it anymore, but because I love it too much. And because I want to preserve that love and respect it for what it has given me over the years. And because I want to make room for new experiences and new adventures in my life. And because I want to spend more time with my family and friends who have supported me and loved me throughout my career.

So this is my farewell speech to Hollywood. To all the people who have worked with me and helped me along the way: Thank you for your collaboration, your guidance, your friendship. To all the people who have watched my films and appreciated my work: Thank you for your attention, your admiration, your criticism. To all the people who have inspired me and taught me: Thank you for your wisdom, your generosity, your example.

You have all been part of my journey as an actor, and you will always be part of my life.

I hope you'll enjoy *Phantom Thread*, and I hope you'll remember me fondly.

Thank you.

	How to Say Goodbye to Hollywood
Introduction	A. Opening remarks and introduction B. Announcing retirement from acting C. Expressing gratitude and respect for the audience
Body	A. Love for acting • Passion for the craft and art of acting • Working with 1. _____ • Connection with the audience B. Demands and sacrifices • Dedication, 2. _____, and commitment required • Impact on physical, mental, and emotional health • Effects on personal life, 3. _____, and privacy C. Selectivity and challenges • Being 4. _____ with roles and projects • Challenging oneself and doing justice to characters • Giving everything to each performance D. Reflection on retirement decision • Fulfilling experience of working on *Phantom Thread* • Realization of diminished energy and enthusiasm • Need for a(n) 5. _____ and exploration of new interests E. Gratitude and farewell
Conclusion	Farewell to Hollywood and final blessings

Activity Four

Choose one of the following topics and deliver a speech on a special occasion with the help of the public speaking skill above.

- ◆ Introducing a guest speaker at a conference
- ◆ Congratulating your colleague on his or her promotion
- ◆ Accepting an award with grace and humility

Section C Further Listening

Activity One

You will hear a talk in a sociology class. Listen and choose the best answer to each question.

1. What is the main proposition of technological determinism?

    A. Technology is shaped by societal influences.

    B. Technology causes social change independent of other societal influences.

    C. Societies can resist technological changes.

    D. Technological innovation comes from nowhere.

2. What is an example of a technology that led to increased literacy rates?

    A. The printing press.

    B. The Internet.

    C. The telephone.

    D. The steam engine.

3. According to technological determinism, what is the significance of whether a technology's impact is positive or negative?

    A. It determines the speed of social change.

    B. It is irrelevant to the theory.

    C. It influences the acceptance of the technology.

    D. It determines the cultural readiness for innovation.

4. How does technological determinism view the resistance of societies to technological changes?

    A. Societies can effectively resist technological changes.

B. Societies cannot resist technological changes.

   C. Societies only resist changes that are perceived as negative.

   D. Societies can resist changes through economic factors.

5. What do opponents of technological determinism argue?

   A. Societies are unable to resist technological changes.

   B. Technological innovation is independent of societal factors.

   C. Technologies are products of their societies.

   D. Societies are always psychologically and culturally ready for technological innovation.

6. What is an example given to support the opposing view of technological determinism?

   A. The invention of perspective in ancient Greece.

   B. The development of the printing press in Germany.

   C. The advent of photography in the 19th century.

   D. The rise of the Internet in modern society.

7. What did opponents of technological determinism argue about the invention of photography?

   A. Society was technologically ready for photography before it was culturally ready.

   B. The invention of photography was a result of a technological breakthrough.

   C. Painters delayed the beginnings of photography through their painting trends.

   D. Photography was embraced as an art form due to its everyday subject matter.

8. What is the main critique offered by opponents of technological determinism?

   A. Technological changes are inevitable and cannot be resisted.

   B. Societies need to be in the right frame of mind for new technologies to take hold.

   C. Technological innovation is solely determined by economic factors.

   D. Societal influences play no role in shaping technology.

9. What is the main agreement between technological determinism and its opponents?

   A. Technology is shaped by cultural factors.

   B. Societal readiness is necessary for technological innovation.

   C. Social change is driven by political events.

   D. Technological change is always positive.

10. What is the main focus of the discussion in the lecture?

    A. The influence of technology on art movements.

    B. The role of culture in technological innovation.

    C. The impact of technology on social change.

    D. The debate between technological determinism and its opponents.

Activity Two

Listen to a lecture in a communications class. Complete the outline by filling in each blank within three words.

Crisis Communications and Public Relations

I. Introduction

Importance of crisis communication in maintaining an organization's 1. _____ and existence

II. Handling crisis situations
- Priority in crisis communication: maintaining credibility and 2. _____
- Consequences of 3. _____ crisis communications
- Importance of communicating correct information to prevent rumors

III. Press release
- Definition—a short 4. _____ explaining the crisis and solutions
- Contents—containing concise information and 5. _____ information

IV. Communicating bad news
- Importance of not keeping bad news a(n) 6. _____
- Controlling the message to present the information in the 7. _____
- Example of a hotel chain's computer 8. _____ and how to turn it into a positive message
- Needing a designated spokesman who is 9. _____ about the company and the crisis
- Needing a team of company experts who specialize in crisis, 10. _____ things

Activity Three

Listen to a passage about the preparation techniques of traditional Chinese medicine and fill in each blank within three words.

Preparation Techniques of Traditional Chinese Medicine

The processing techniques of Chinese medicine refer to the traditional methods and techniques of processing medicinal materials into medicinal pieces ready for decoction under the guidance of traditional Chinese medicinal theories as required by medical doctors.

The processing of traditional Chinese medicine has a long history in China, making its appearance in many 1. _____ from pre-Qin period. In the period of the 2. _____

Unit 16
Digital Darwinism

Dynasties, a pharmacologist wrote *Lei Gong's Treatise on Preparation of Materia Medica*, the 3. _____ book in China about the processing of traditional Chinese medicine, which has recorded 4. _____ methods and techniques for medicine processing and exerted a great influence on later generations.

Over the past thousands of years, Chinese people have 5. _____ quite a large number of processing methods and techniques and developed a set of 6. _____ for processing medicine. The processing methods which are still in wide use include stir-frying, 7. _____, forging and stewing, and the tools are also of a rich variety, featuring such traditional hand tools as the 8. _____, slicer knife, file, hammer, and mill groove. With the development of science and technology, certain machines are now applied to process Chinese medicine, such as the pulverators used for 9. _____ and the cutter machines for making pieces.

In 10. _____, the preparation techniques of traditional Chinese medicine were added to the list of China's National Intangible Cultural Heritage.

(Text A=A; Text B=B)

A

abundant	Unit11B
accrue	Unit16A
address	Unit13B
adept	Unit9B
afflict	Unit9B
aggravate	Unit13A
agile	Unit16A
algorithmic	Unit13A
algorithm	Unit14B
altered	Unit15B
antenatal	Unit5A
architect	Unit3B
articulate	Unit15B
aural	Unit4B
authentication	Unit10A
authoritative	Unit15B

B

backbone	Unit10B
bargain	Unit5A
bedrock	Unit3A
belie	Unit8A
binary	Unit2A
bias	Unit13A
biochemistry	Unit12A
biopsy	Unit12A
bit	Unit2A
Bogota	Unit16B
brainchild	Unit15A
breakneck	Unit10B

C

cancerous	Unit12A
carjacker	Unit12A
celebrity	Unit14A
certificate	Unit7B
clinical	Unit9B
compatible	Unit2B
compelling	Unit4A
component	Unit2B
compound	Unit16A

conference	Unit1B	**E**	
configure	Unit6B	effectively	Unit1A
conservatively	Unit5A	embed	Unit8A
considerable	Unit1A	enablement	Unit10B
constraint	Unit5B	encrypt	Unit7B
consultant	Unit3B	encryption	Unit8A
contemporary	Unit5B	endurance	Unit5B
continuous	Unit16B	enthusiast	Unit16B
convergent	Unit14A	epidemic	Unit9B
conversational	Unit15A	existential	Unit14A
convert	Unit15A	expertise	Unit3B
corporate	Unit4B	exponential	Unit16A
correlation	Unit9A	extraversion	Unit9A
counterargument	Unit14A		
counterfeit	Unit8A	**F**	
cusp	Unit10B	fallout	Unit6B
		feedback	Unit12B
D		flaw	Unit6B
debug	Unit2B	flexibility	Unit5A
decent	Unit1B	flop	Unit9A
deepfake	Unit14B	forum	Unit12B
deliver	Unit1A	framework	Unit2B
demonstrate	Unit3B	full-blown	Unit9A
demote	Unit13A		
deployment	Unit11B	**G**	
desensitize	Unit8A	gauge	Unit15A
developer	Unit11A	generative	Unit14B
discriminatory	Unit15B	gut	Unit6B
disregard.	Unit6A		
dissident	Unit7B	**H**	
distinguish	Unit14B	Hacktivist	Unit7B
distracted	Unit9A	Hadoop	Unit12B
divine	Unit16A	hands-on	Unit4B
documentary	Unit9B	haphazardly	Unit6A
dopamine	Unit9A	harness	Unit12B
		high-profile	Unit14A

Glossary

hot-desking	Unit11A
humanity	Unit14A
hybrid	Unit5B
hypothetical	Unit14A

I

immense	Unit1A
inequality	Unit5A
infraction	Unit8A
infrastructure	Unit3A
infringe	Unit9B
inkwell	Unit12A
installation	Unit7A
integrate	Unit4A
intrinsically	Unit14A
investigate	Unit1A
irrigation	Unit10A

J

jeopardy	Unit8A
junkie	Unit9B

K

kinesthetic	Unit4B

L

labor	Unit11B
laboratory	Unit1A
leverage	Unit3A
linear	Unit16A
looting	Unit8A

M

malicious	Unit8B
malware	Unit8B
masculine	Unit5B
massive	Unit4A
melding	Unit10B
metabolic	Unit16A
metaverse	Unit14B
microscope	Unit12A
militarized	Unit14A
military	Unit3A
mindset	Unit1B
modality	Unit4B
modular	Unit4B
modulation	Unit2A
momentum	Unit2B
motive	Unit7B
multidisciplinary	Unit13B
Munich	Unit16B

N

nasty	Unit6B
neural	Unit6A
neutral	Unit13A
niche	Unit4A
notoriety	Unit7A
novelty	Unit10A

O

occupation	Unit11B
on-demand	Unit4B
oppression	Unit13A
optimal	Unit4B
optional	Unit11A
orientation	Unit13B
oscillate	Unit2A
outperform	Unit12B

P

pediatrics	Unit9B
penalize	Unit13A

penetration	Unit16A	savvy	Unit7A
perpetuate	Unit13A	scalable	Unit4B
persistence	Unit5B	scenario	Unit11B
plausible	Unit7B	scroll	Unit9A
plausible-sounding	Unit15A	scrub	Unit15A
pop up	Unit6A	sentiment	Unit12B
potential	Unit5A	Seoul	Unit16B
practical	Unit1A	server	Unit6B
prevailing	Unit1B	simulator	Unit14B
privilege	Unit5B	snippet	Unit15A
projection	Unit3B	soothe	Unit9B
prove	Unit1A	sophisticated	Unit15A
proximity	Unit10A	sponsor	Unit1A
		spotty	Unit7A
		SSL	Unit7B

Q

quill	Unit12A

		stab	Unit15B
		staggering	Unit7A

R

		stakeholder	Unit12A
random	Unit6A	status quo	Unit6A
real-time	Unit10A	streamline	Unit11A
reflexively	Unit9B	string	Unit2A
regardless	Unit11A	stringent	Unit8B
reliability	Unit2B	subsequent	Unit13B
remote	Unit11A	supremacy	Unit13A
render	Unit14B	synthesis	Unit14B
render into	Unit12A		
repercussion	Unit8A		

T

representative	Unit11B		
retention	Unit4B	tablet	Unit10A
rhetoric	Unit5B	tackle	Unit5A
router	Unit6B	take into account	Unit1B
		telltale	Unit12A

S

		tenfold	Unit12B
sample	Unit4A	therapy	Unit9B
sandwich	Unit15B	titan	Unit14A
Sao Paulo	Unit16B	totalitarian	Unit7B
		transform	Unit5A

Glossary

transistor	Unit2A	validate	Unit3B
tricky	Unit7A	validation	Unit14B
troubleshoot	Unit3A	verify	Unit13B
trove	Unit4A	vertical	Unit3B
trustworthy	Unit7B	volt	Unit2A
		voltage	Unit2A

U

ultimately	Unit14A
undermine	Unit10B
unnerving	Unit8A

V

vacancy	Unit1B

W

weed	Unit15B
weigh	Unit11B
whopping	Unit6A
workflow	Unit14B